LINCOLNSHIRE
COUNCIL

www.northlincs.gov.uk

TH
CON

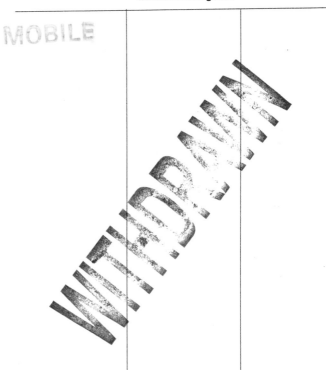

To renew this item, log onto **www.northlincs.gov.uk/
librarycatalogue,** click on *borrower information* and follow the
prompts. You will need to quote your ticket number and PIN to
use this service.

About the Author

Michael Osiris Snuffin is a ceremonial magician, a practitioner of the Golden Dawn, Thelemic, and Chaos Magick traditions. He is an initiate of the Ordo Templi Orientis (OTO) and the founder and Chief Adept of the Temple of Light and Darkness, a group of operative magicians united to work through the Golden Dawn system of initiation in accordance with the Law of Thelema.

Snuffin is a longtime student of magick, Thelema, and the Thoth tarot. A graduate of the Evergreen State College, he lives in Seattle.

Please visit his personal website at www.hermetic.com/osiris/index.htm.

To Write to the Author

If you wish to contact the author or would like more information about this book, please write to the author in care of Llewellyn Worldwide and we will forward your request. Both the author and publisher appreciate hearing from you and learning of your enjoyment of this book and how it has helped you. Llewellyn Worldwide cannot guarantee that every letter written to the author can be answered, but all will be forwarded. Please write to:

Michael Osiris Snuffin
℅ Llewellyn Worldwide
2143 Wooddale Drive, Dept. 978-0-7387-1192-8
Woodbury, MN 55125-2989, U.S.A.

Please enclose a self-addressed stamped envelope for reply,
or $1.00 to cover costs. If outside the USA, enclose
an international postal reply coupon.

Many of Llewellyn's authors have websites with additional information and resources. For more information, please visit our website at www.llewellyn.com.

THE THOTH COMPANION

The Key to the
True Symbolic Meaning of the
Thoth Tarot

MICHAEL OSIRIS SNUFFIN

Llewellyn Publications
Woodbury, Minnesota

First Edition
First Printing, 2007

Book design by Steffani Sawyer
Cover design by Lisa Novak
Editing by Brett Fechheimer
Interior diagrams courtesy of the Llewellyn Art Department
Tarot card illustrations from Aleister Crowley Thoth Tarot® reproduced by permission of AGM AGMüller, CH-8212 Neuhausen, Switzerland. ©AGM AGMüller / OTO. Further reproduction prohibited.
Llewellyn is a registered trademark of Llewellyn Worldwide, Ltd.

Library of Congress Cataloging-in-Publication Data
Snuffin, Michael Osiris.
    The Thoth companion: the key to the true symbolic meaning of the Thoth tarot / Michael
    Osiris Snuffin. — 1st ed.
        p.   cm.
    Includes bibliographical references and index.
    ISBN: 978-0-7387-1192-8
1. Tarot I. Title.

    BF1879.T2S68 2007
    133.3'2424—dc22   2007029072

Llewellyn Worldwide does not participate in, endorse, or have any authority or responsibility concerning private business transactions between our authors and the public.
    All mail addressed to the author is forwarded but the publisher cannot, unless specifically instructed by the author, give out an address or phone number.
    Any Internet references contained in this work are current at publication time, but the publisher cannot guarantee that a specific location will continue to be maintained. Please refer to the publisher's website for links to authors' websites and other sources.

Llewellyn Publications
A Division of Llewellyn Worldwide, Ltd.
2143 Wooddale Drive, Dept. 978-0-7387-1192-8
Woodbury, Minnesota 55125-2989, U.S.A.
www.llewellyn.com

Printed in the United States of America

Other Books by Michael Osiris Snuffin

Practical Goetic Magick (self-published)

Contents

Contents

Introduction

Aleister Crowley's Thoth tarot is one of the most popular and enigmatic tarot decks of the modern age. A longtime student of the tarot and the Qabala, Crowley took the design and structure of the tarot from the Golden Dawn system of magick and revised it in accordance with his own magickal system of Thelema. This marriage of the two systems, skillfully painted by Lady Frieda Harris, is vibrant and complex. Its appeal reaches far beyond the students of Thelema and the Golden Dawn systems.

The Book of Thoth was the last major work of Crowley's prolific writing career, published only three years before his death. It is a record of Crowley's extensive magickal knowledge and experience, and it is a guide to the history and structure of the esoteric tarot containing detailed descriptions of the cards. *The Book of Thoth* still stands today as one of the most advanced textbooks on the tarot ever published.

At the same time, Crowley's description of the symbolism of the Thoth tarot is often confusing and sometimes incomplete. *The Book of Thoth* assumes a great deal of knowledge on the part of the reader, especially concerning the Golden Dawn and Thelemic magickal systems. Obscure references abound in the text, and there is no bibliography in *The Book of Thoth* to fall back upon for answers. *The Book of Thoth* also glosses over many of the symbolic details of the Thoth tarot and sometimes even neglects to mention symbols within the cards.

The purpose of *The Thoth Companion* is to explore the symbolism of the Thoth tarot and provide a comprehensive analysis of the deck. Using material from the Golden Dawn and Thelemic systems as the basis for analysis, this book will show how the symbols in each card define and shape the meaning of the card as a whole. In addition, it will reveal the complex correspondences and elusive secrets that Crowley encoded within the Thoth tarot. Chapter 1 of this book examines the trumps of the deck and includes an introduction that discusses Crowley's primary sources for the design and symbolism of the trump cards. Chapter 2 decodes the complicated symbolic framework of the court cards presented in the Golden Dawn's *Book T* and adopted by Crowley in the Thoth tarot. Chapter 3 analyzes the symbolism of the suit cards of the Thoth tarot. Chapter 4 gives instructions for tarot divination and includes exercises to help you learn the meanings of the cards and develop your intuition. Tables of symbol sets and correspondences are included in an appendix.

The tarot speaks to us in the language of symbols. Those who use the Thoth deck for divination will discover that knowledge of the symbolism of the cards will increase the clarity and depth of their tarot readings. I have included my own interpretations of the cards, which are derived from their symbols and based on my experience as a tarot reader.

The material in this book is especially useful in pathworking exercises. Understanding the symbols and their purpose within the trumps will assist the magician in interacting with them in a vision and aid him in interpretation. Studying the symbolism of the Thoth deck will help the neophyte magician learn and apply the many Qabalistic correspondences of the Golden Dawn and Thelema. This book also serves as a basic introduction to the Thelemic concepts and symbolism found in Crowley's works.

Like *The Book of Thoth*, this book is not an introductory text on the tarot. Familiarity with the symbol sets listed in the appendix is suggested for full comprehension of what is presented here. Many of the magick and tarot books on the shelf define and discuss these symbol sets; *Self-Initiation into the Golden Dawn Tradition* by Chic and Sandra Tabatha Cicero is highly recommended. A little preparation will lead to much greater understanding.

The Thoth Companion is the key to the true symbolic meaning of the Thoth deck. May it assist you in your pursuit of the Great Work.

Frater Osiris
Seattle, Washington
November 2006

The Trumps

The symbolism of the twenty-two trumps of the Thoth deck is derived from two primary sources: the Golden Dawn and the works of Aleister Crowley.

The Golden Dawn provided the framework for Crowley's early studies of the occult tarot and its correspondences. This knowledge was given to the Adeptus Minor of the Golden Dawn in the form of *Book T*, a document that laid out a specific symbolic plan for the seventy-eight cards of the tarot. *Book T* actually offers little information on the trumps, giving only the most basic correspondences that were already revealed in the earlier grade of Practicus. The actual Golden Dawn trumps were given to the Adept to copy by hand for personal use.

We know that Crowley was familiar with *Book T*, not only because he was an Adeptus Minor, but also because he published the document in 1912 as part of *The Equinox, Volume 1, Number 8*. While *Book T* provides little information on the trumps, it does offer detailed descriptions of the court cards and the suit cards that influenced the design of Crowley's own minor arcana.

More detailed descriptions of the trump symbolism and meaning are given in the initiation rituals of the Golden Dawn. The initiatory grades of the Golden Dawn correspond to the lower Sephiroth of the Tree of Life. As the candidate advances through the outer order grades, he symbolically ascends the Tree of Life from Malkuth to Tiphareth. The lower paths of the Tree of Life are revealed to the initiate in the form of the corresponding tarot trumps (see table 1).

Table 1: Grade-trump correspondences

Grade	Sephira	Trumps
Zelator	Malkuth	N/A
Theoricus	Yesod	Universe
Practicus	Hod	Aeon, Sun
Philosophus	Netzach	Moon, Star, Tower
Portal	N/A	Devil, Art, Death
Adeptus Minor	Tiphareth	N/A

Aleister Crowley was an initiate of Adeptus Minor Grade in the Golden Dawn, and therefore he had access to the Golden Dawn trump information. He would have also had a good understanding of Qabala, astrology, and alchemy, having been instructed in and tested on these subjects in the lower grades.

Crowley was a prolific writer, and many aspects of his trump designs are derived from his most significant published works. Here is a brief look at the primary sources.

The Book of the Law (*Liber AL*) is probably the most important book penned by Crowley in his lifetime. Received in Cairo in 1904, it ushered in the Law of Thelema and the Aeon of Horus. Crowley's whole life changed when he became the herald of the New Aeon and the prophet of Thelema, and *The Book of the Law* was an integral part of his later works. *The Law Is for All*, Crowley's commentary on *Liber AL*, is an especially useful reference on Thelemic symbolism.

In this book, citations of *The Book of the Law* are given in the format (AL II:73), where the Roman numeral refers to the chapter and the following number refers to the verse.

The Book of the Law initiated a fundamental change in the attributions of two tarot trumps with the statement "Tzaddi is not the Star" (AL I:57). After much contemplation, Crowley realized that the Hebrew letter Tzaddi is attributed to the Emperor, and he assigned the letter Hé to the Star. This manipulation changes the placement of the two trumps on the Tree of Life.

Thelemic symbolism is abundant in the Thoth trumps. For example, the Hierophant shows the gods of the three Thelemic Aeons—Isis, Osiris, and Horus. Lust shows Babalon and the Beast conjoined. The Star depicts Nuit, who is "Infinite Space, and the Infinite Stars thereof" (AL 1:22). Crowley's most radical divergence from the traditional design is found in the Aeon, which he redesigned to resemble the Stèle of Revealing, an icon of the New Aeon of Horus.

The Vision and the Voice (Liber 418) is another source of inspiration for the design and symbolism of the Thoth trumps. It consists of documentation of Crowley's visions of the thirty Enochian Aethyrs, text that is rife with references to tarot and Qabala. Crowley's commentary and analysis of these visions has been recently republished as *The Equinox, Vol. 4, No. 2*, a useful tool for decoding some of Crowley's more obscure symbolism. The Chariot, Adjustment, and Fortune each play a significant role in separate visions.

Liber Aleph (Liber 111) is a series of letters on magickal philosophy written for Crowley's magickal son, Frater Achad. It includes commentary on many aspects of the trumps, including the Fool and the Devil. *Liber Aleph* also expounds upon the Powers of the Sphinx, found in the Hierophant, the Chariot, and the Universe—and it explains the Tripartite Scorpio of Death.

777 is an essential compendium of Qabalistic and Hermetic correspondences. Many of the symbols found within the Thoth tarot can be defined by looking them up in the tables of *777*. Another useful resource published in *777* is "Sepher Sephiroth," a Qabalistic dictionary used to determine correspondences through the use of gematria.

Liber ABA (Book Four, parts I–IV) is Crowley's magnum opus of magick. It includes material previously published as *Book Four* and *Magick in Theory and Practice* as well as an impressive collection of Crowley's shorter works. Some of the included Libers also expound upon the tarot, especially the Thelemic Holy Books *Liber Cheth* and *Liber A'ash*.

This list would not be complete without mentioning *The Book of Thoth*, Crowley's own guide to the Thoth deck. This is the authoritative work on the subject, and no study of the Thoth tarot deck would be complete without it.

Figure 1: The Tree of Life with Tarot Attributions

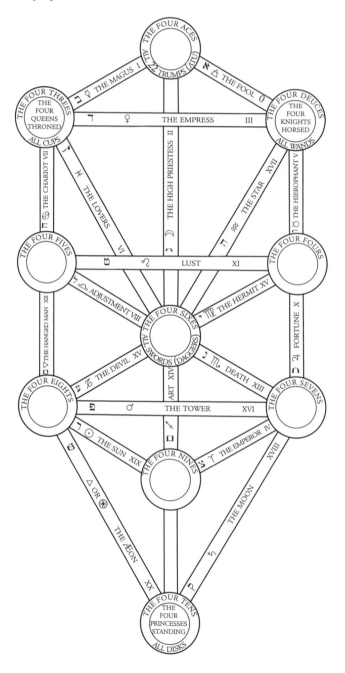

The Tarot Trumps and the Hebrew Alphabet

The Golden Dawn assigned specific correspondences between the twenty-two trumps, the twenty-two letters of the Hebrew alphabet, and attributions of an element, planet, or zodiacal sign (see table 2). Two corrections were made to these correspondences. The Golden Dawn switched the path attributions of Justice (renamed "Adjustment" in the Thoth deck) and Strength (Lust) to align them with the zodiacal attributions of Libra and Leo respectively. Crowley later switched the attributions of the Emperor and the Star to correspond with the Hebrew letters Tzaddi and Hé as dictated in *The Book of the Law*, a change that balanced the correction made by the Golden Dawn.[1]

The Aeon and the Universe bear the dual attributions of Fire/Spirit and Saturn/Earth respectively. This reflects the fact that the ancients originally believed that the universe consisted of the three elements of Fire, Water, and Air; Spirit and Earth were later additions to this elemental system.

Table 2: Primary Attributions of the Trumps

Trump	Hebrew Letter	Value	Name of Letter	Meaning	Attribution	Path
0. The Fool	א	1	Aleph	Ox	Air	11
I. The Magus	ב	2	Beth	House	Mercury	12
II. The Priestess	ג	3	Gimel	Camel	Moon	13
III. The Empress	ד	4	Daleth	Door	Venus	14
IV. The Emperor	צ	90, 900	Tzaddi	Fish Hook	Aries	28
V. The Hiero-phant	ו	6	Vau	Nail	Taurus	16
VI. The Lovers	ז	7	Zayin	Sword	Gemini	17
VII. The Chariot	ח	8	Cheth	Fence	Cancer	18
VIII. Adjustment	ל	30	Lamed	Ox-goad	Libra	22
IX. The Hermit	י	10	Yod	Hand	Virgo	20
X. Fortune	כ, ך	20, 500	Kaph	Palm, Fist	Jupiter	21
XI. Lust	ט	9	Teth	Snake	Leo	19

---

1. Crowley, *The Book of Thoth*, 10–11.

XII. The Hanged Man	מ	40, 600	Mem	Water	Water	23
XIII. Death	נ, ן	50, 700	Nun	Fish	Scorpio	24
XIV. Art	ס	60	Samekh	Prop	Sagittarius	25
XV. The Devil	ע	70	Ayin	Eye	Capricorn	26
XVI. The Tower	פ, ף	80, 800	Pé	Mouth	Mars	27
XVII. The Star	ה	5	Hé	Window	Aquarius	15
XVIII. The Moon	ק	100	Qoph	Back of Head	Pisces	29
XIX. The Sun	ר	200	Resh	Head, Face	Sun	30
XX. The Aeon	ש	300	Shin	Tooth	Fire, Spirit	31
XXI. The Universe	ת	400	Tau	Cross	Saturn, Earth	32

Color plays an important part in the symbolism of the Thoth tarot, as the color of a symbol often indicates its Qabalistic correspondences. Each Sephira and path on the Tree of Life is associated with four colors, one for each of the Four Worlds (see table 3). The Aeon and the Universe have two color attributions because they each have an additional elemental attribution. In the Thoth tarot, the Four Color Scales are used to signify the energy and the influence of the Sephira or trump with which they are connected.

Table 3: The Four Color Scales

Sephira	Atziluth (Knight Scale)	Briah (Queen Scale)	Yetzirah (Prince Scale)	Assiah (Princess Scale)
Kether	Brilliance	White brilliance	White brilliance	White, flecked gold
Chokmah	Pure soft blue	Gray	Blue pearl gray, like mother-of-pearl	White flecked red, blue, and yellow
Binah	Crimson	Black	Dark brown	Gray, flecked pink
Chesed	Deep violet	Blue	Deep purple	Deep azure, flecked yellow
Geburah	Orange	Scarlet red	Bright scarlet	Red, flecked black
Tiphareth	Clear pink rose	Yellow (gold)	Rich salmon	Gold amber

Netzach	Amber	Emerald	Bright yellow-green	Olive, flecked gold
Hod	Violet	Orange	Red-russet	Yellowish-brown, flecked white
Yesod	Indigo	Violet	Very dark purple	Citrine, flecked azure
Malkuth	Yellow	Citrine, olive, russet, and black saltire	As Queen Scale, but gold-flecked black	Black rayed with yellow

Trump	Atziluth (Knight Scale)	Briah (Queen Scale)	Yetzirah (Prince Scale)	Assiah (Princess Scale)
0. The Fool (Air)	Bright pale yellow	Sky blue	Blue emerald green	Emerald, flecked gold
I. The Magus (Mercury)	Yellow	Purple	Gray	Indigo, rayed violet
II. The Priestess (Moon)	Blue	Silver	Cold pale blue	Silver, rayed sky blue
III. The Empress (Venus)	Emerald green	Sky blue	Early spring green	Bright rose or cerise, rayed pale green
IV. The Emperor (Aries)	Scarlet	Red	Brilliant flame	Glowing red
V. The Hierophant (Taurus)	Red orange	Deep indigo	Deep warm olive	Rich brown
VI. The Lovers (Gemini)	Orange	Pale mauve	New yellow leather	Reddish gray, inclined to mauve
VII. The Chariot (Cancer)	Amber	Maroon	Rich bright russet	Dark greenish brown
VIII. Adjustment (Libra)	Emerald green	Blue	Deep blue-green	Pale green
IX. The Hermit (Virgo)	Green (yellowish)	Slate gray	Green gray	Plum
X. Fortune (Jupiter)	Violet	Blue	Rich purple	Bright blue, rayed yellow
XI. Lust (Leo)	Yellow (greenish)	Deep purple	Gray	Reddish amber

XII. The Hanged Man (Water)	Deep blue	Sea green	Deep olive-green	White, flecked purple
XIII. Death (Scorpio)	Green blue	Dull brown	Very dark brown	Vivid indigo brown
XIV. Art (Sagittarius)	Blue	Yellow	Green	Dark vivid blue
XV. The Devil (Capricorn)	Indigo	Black	Blue-black	Cold dark gray, nearing black
XVI. The Tower (Mars)	Scarlet	Red	Venetian red	Bright red, rayed azure or purple
XVII. The Star (Aquarius)	Violet	Sky blue	Bluish mauve	White, tinged purple
XVIII. The Moon (Pisces)	Crimson (ultraviolet)	Buff, flecked silver-white	Light translucent pinkish brown	Stone color
XIX. The Sun (Sun)	Orange	Gold yellow	Rich amber	Amber, rayed red
XX. The Aeon (Fire)	Glowing orange scarlet	Vermillion	Scarlet, flecked gold	Vermillion, flecked emerald and crimson
XX. The Aeon (Spirit)	White, merging into gray	Deep purple, nearly black	The seven prismatic colors	White, red, yellow, blue, black
XXI. The Universe (Earth)	Citrine, olive, russet, and black	Amber	Dark brown	Black, flecked yellow
XXI. The Universe (Saturn)	Indigo	Black	Blue-black	Black, flecked yellow

The five Elements also have basic color attributions.

Element	Color
Spirit	White
Fire	Red
Water	Blue
Air	Yellow
Earth	Green or black

The Fool is a glyph of the infinite creative potential of the universe. This is the first of the trumps, and it signifies the beginning of the Great Work.

The Fool is crowned with a diamond, the stone of Kether. The rainbow-colored halo surrounding his head symbolizes the enlightenment he receives from Kether. The background behind the Fool is the yellow of Air spotted with white diamonds, symbols of Kether.

The Fool's skin is yellow, the color of Air. The horns on his head symbolize creative force. His clothing is green, the color of the fertile Earth, and his shoes are yellow-gold—the color of the Sun, the creative light of life that warms and nourishes the Earth. The Sun is connected with the element of Air through the attribution of the Vau (Air) of the Tetragrammaton to Tiphareth (Sun).

The symbol of the Sun is placed at the Fool's root chakra to signify human consciousness at its most basic level, the newborn child's need for survival and security. The Sun also symbolizes the creative potential within the genitals.

A rainbow-hued spiral circles the Fool three times, symbolizing Ain Soph Aur, the Three Negative Veils of Existence above Kether on the Tree of Life. The spiral forms the fertile womb of Nuit that gestates Harpocrates, the Lord of Silence. In this context, the spiral is also the umbilical cord, attached to the Fool at his heart chakra, which is the link between the higher and lower energies of the chakra system.

A dove, a vulture, and a butterfly fly toward the Fool's heart. The dove signifies the descent of spirit into matter. Twenty rays of light emanate from the

0. The Fool

Hebrew Letter
Aleph

Meaning
Ox

Attribution
Air

Path
11th

Connects
Kether and Chokmah

dove, the numerical value of Yod when spelled out in full. The dove, which is attributed to Venus, is a feminine symbol, and the rays of light indicate the masculine influence of Yod. Therefore the dove is a sexually complete symbol, a hermaphrodite.

The vulture represents Mut, the Egyptian Mother-goddess and consort of Amun at Thebes. Mut, whose name means "Mother," was believed to possess both the male and female powers of reproduction, and was therefore considered to be the creator of all things. This had its basis in the belief that there were no male vultures, and the female vultures were impregnated by the winds (Air).

The butterfly is a symbol of Air. The butterfly also represents the soul; in this trump it represents the soul entering the unborn babe in the womb.

Leading this spiraling procession is an unusual caduceus crowned with a pinecone and having a sword blade for a shaft. The caduceus and the sword are symbols of Air. The caduceus is a symbol of creative energy. The pinecone alludes to the Thyrsus, a pinecone-topped staff associated with Dionysus.[2] The Thyrsus is a symbol of creative energy.

A grapevine sprouts from the Fool's heart chakra, identifying him with Dionysus and Bacchus. Wine is a vehicle of madness and ecstasy, especially in connection with the myth of Dionysus.

Suspended from the grapevine is a sack of coins inscribed with astrological symbols. The Sun is at the center surrounded by the six ancient planets, which in turn are encircled by the belt of the zodiac. This represents the influence of the macrocosm, the body of Nuit. The planets and signs are the powers potentially available to the Fool.

The Fool holds a firebrand or flaming pinecone in his left hand—a symbol of raw, creative fire. In his right hand he bears a cup, pouring its contents on the ground below. The base of the cup is a pyramid, symbolic of the phallus, while the bowl is symbolic of the womb. The sexual organs are in turn symbols of Chokmah and Binah, and the symbols flank the diamond crown of Kether. (The projection of the Tree of Life on this trump can be taken even further, with the Sun at the center of the card representing Tiphareth and the crocodile as Malkuth.) Amidst the whorls of air, the

---

2. The Thyrsus is also found in the Queen of Wands.

fire arches over the Fool to unite with the cup. This symbolism is analogous with the unification of the lance and cup that resolves the Hermetic Marriage.[3]

Below the Fool is a curious arrangement of flowers. The uppermost flower is a white rose; its white color links it with Kether. The rose is a symbol of Air in the initiation rituals of the Golden Dawn. Hanging from the stem of the rose are four lilies. The lily is attributed to Binah (Saturn), Malkuth, and Virgo as a symbol of the purity of the Earth. The three smaller lilies have four petals each, while the large lily has five petals for a total of seventeen petals; together they are representative of the sixteen sub-elements crowned by Spirit.

Crowley describes the lilies as "the benediction of three flowers in one."[4] This is a reference to the Final Hé of the Tetragrammaton, the Daughter attributed to the element of Earth, who is the product of the Father, Mother, and Son. Thus, all four letters of the Tetragrammaton are represented in this card: the firebrand as Yod, the cup as the Primal Hé, the rose as Vau, and the lilies as the Final Hé.

The infants embracing below the flower arrangement also represent the Vau and Final Hé. These infants mature to become Ra-Hoor-Khuit and Harpocrates, the "solar twins" found in the Lovers and the Sun.

A tiger and a crocodile threaten the Fool. The tiger is attributed to Leo, and it is reddish amber, the color of Leo in Assiah. The tiger represents the passion and lust that may distract the Fool from the Great Work.

The crocodile is attributed to Saturn as the devourer.[5] As a symbol of Saturn, it indicates the influence of the universe, the end of the cycle of trumps that the Fool initiates. The crocodile is also Sebek, the Egyptian god who represents the destructive power of the Sun. In Egyptian myth, Sebek hid among the banks of the Nile, waiting to devour Harpocrates.

Interpretation

As the first of the trumps, the Fool symbolizes creation, birth, and the beginning of an endeavor. The crown of Kether signifies wisdom in spiritual matters, while the numerous symbols of Air signify success in mental matters. New ideas arise, poten-

---

3. See the description of the trumps the Lovers and Art.
4. Crowley, Aleister, *The Book of Thoth* (York Beach, ME: Samuel Weiser, 1993), 69.
5. Saturn is the Roman name for Cronus, the titan who swallowed his own children because he feared they would overthrow him as the king of the gods.

tial is realized, and plans are made when the Fool appears in a spread. However, the wisdom and potential of the Fool only become manifest in the trumps that follow, particularly in the Magus.

The Fool reversed indicates the futility and insanity of acting on these ideas without a realistic assessment of the means to implement them. Thus, the tiger and crocodile that threaten him indicate folly in emotional and material matters. The pinecone and the grapevine of Dionysus signify the mania that occurs when a person is divorced from reality.

The Magus is a glyph of the harnessed and directed will, embodied in the image of the archetypal magician Hermes Trismegistus.

Many Thoth tarot decks come with three different versions of the Magus, allowing the owner to select the trump he finds most desirable. While the three trumps are different in appearance, the general symbolism remains constant, so most of the analysis that follows applies to all three versions. The specific version of the Magus discussed here is the most common of the three and is printed in the back of *The Book of Thoth*.[6]

The Magus is naked to show that he is androgynous. As with the Fool above, the path of Beth originates from the absolute unity of Kether and therefore has no separate sexual characteristics. His skin is yellow and gray, Mercury in Atziluth and Yetzirah.

The Magus juggles eight tools that he uses to accomplish his will: the disk, the censer, the Wand of Double Power, the stylus or pen, the scroll, the Winged Egg, the cup, and the dagger.

The disk, dagger, cup, and censer are the four elemental weapons of the Magus. Note that the censer has replaced the traditional wand as the elemental weapon of Fire. Used in conjunction with the cup, the censer represents the consecrating Fire in the Neophyte Ceremony of the Golden Dawn and also in the Gnostic Mass. The Winged Egg represents the fifth element of Spirit.

The Wand of Double Power is a symbol of the energy and power of Horus, the Lord of the New Aeon. It symbolizes the harmonizing energy of the

I. The Magus

Hebrew Letter
Beth

Meaning
House

Attribution
Mercury

Path
12th

Connects
Kether and Binah

The Magus

---

6. Crowley, *The Book of Thoth*, 225.

Sun and Tiphareth, and its function is to unite opposites under one will. This wand is also the Phoenix Wand of the Adeptus Minor of the Golden Dawn, where it is a symbol of resurrection.

The Stylus and Scroll are the implements of Thoth, the Egyptian god of writing, wisdom, and magick. Thoth created the hieroglyphs and was the celestial scribe. Writing preserves memories and knowledge, and it is a tool for communication and education; it is an expression of the intellect and the will.

Behind the Magus is the caduceus—the traditional Wand of Mercury, a symbol of creative force and energy. The serpents represent the positive and negative currents of energy harnessed for the purpose of creation. The serpents are purple and yellow, Mercury in Atziluth and Briah.

The serpents coil around the shaft of the caduceus, forming a vertical lemniscate—the symbol of infinity that appears above the head of the Magus in the traditional design of the trump. The lemniscate signifies omniscience. The serpent on the left wears the throne-shaped headdress of Isis, which is associated with Binah, the Great Mother. The serpent on the right wears a simple crown, a symbol of Kether. This symbolism reflects that the Magus connects Kether with Binah. Likewise, the white light of Kether shines behind the Magus, and below him is the darkness of Binah.

The head of the caduceus is a winged phallus. In the center of the caduceus is a blue dove representative of Spirit and the influence of Kether descending from the heavens. The dove is also sacred to Venus, who in the tarot is the Empress, the Fertile Mother. Therefore the phallic caduceus also contains within itself the feminine principle, and is thus sexually complete. The caduceus is outlined in yellow, the color of Air, the Vau of the Tetragrammaton that is the product of the union of the Yod and Primal Hé.

The Magus wears the winged sandals of Hermes, the messenger of the gods in Greek mythology. The sandal strap is a serpent, as it bears the same pattern as the serpents of the caduceus. The sandal strap by its shape and by its nature suggests the ankh, the Egyptian symbol of eternal life; likewise the serpent, which sheds its skin to be made anew, is also a symbol of eternal life. The sandal strap also symbolizes the fifth Power of the Sphinx, to Go.[7]

---

7. The five Powers of the Sphinx are discussed in the description of the Hierophant.

Below the Magus is the Cynocephalus Ape, which is associated with Thoth. Crowley describes the relationship between Thoth and the Cynocephalus Ape as antagonistic, claiming that the role of the Ape is to distort the word of Thoth.[8] However, in the Egyptian Book of the Dead, the Cynocephalus Ape is depicted as the highly intelligent companion of Thoth who assists him in the Weighing of the Heart in the Hall of Judgment.[9]

The Ape is a baboon, an animal attributed to Thoth by the ancient Egyptians. The Ape raises his fist in the air, alluding to the letter Kaph (which means "fist") and the trump Fortune, where the Cynocephalus Ape represents alchemical Mercury.

Interpretation

In a reading, the Magus fulfills Crowley's definition of magick: "the science and art of causing change to occur in conformity with will."[10] The Wand of Double Power symbolizes the will of the magician. The caduceus is indicative of the creative force of the directed will that causes change in the world around us. Mastery and skill (each being both a science and an art) are indicated by the five elemental weapons, the tools used to manipulate the terrestrial universe. The stylus and scroll of Thoth symbolize writing, communication, and education, while the winged sandals of Hermes symbolize messages and travel. Commerce and business, qualities of Mercury, are also meanings of this trump.

When the Magus is reversed, the Cynocephalus Ape distorts the qualities listed above. The will is weak, ineffectual, and unfocused. It signifies a lack of skill or a person who claims to have skills they do not actually possess. Miscommunication, slander, rumors, and gossip are indicated. The negative qualities of Mercury, thievery and trickery, are also present.

---

8. Crowley, *The Book of Thoth*, 72.
9. Budge, E. A. Wallis, *The Gods of the Egyptians,* volume 1 (New York: Dover, 1969), 20–21.
10. Crowley, Aleister, *Liber ABA*, Book 4, parts I–V (York Beach, ME: Samuel Weiser, 2000), 126.

II. The High Priestess

Hebrew Letter
Gimel

Meaning
Camel

Attribution
The Moon

Path
13th

Connects
Kether and Tiphareth

The Priestess is a glyph of purity, aspiration, and esotericism.

The Priestess wears the Crown of Isis, a lunar disk set between a pair of horns that symbolizes the waxing, full, and waning phases of the Moon. The Crown of Isis signifies the idea of cyclical change and flow that is associated with the Moon. The throne, which is associated with Isis as the hieroglyph of her name, is a symbol of stability. Taken together, these symbols of Isis illustrate the aphorism that "change is stability."

Suspended from her crown are seven crescents of increasing size, seven being the number of Venus. Venus is the Empress, which depicts Isis the Eternal Mother, and the trump corresponds to the path of Daleth that crosses the path of Gimel above the Abyss. The eyes of the Priestess are masked with the symbol of infinity, signifying her omniscience.

The veil that conceals the Priestess is also a rainbow, an ethereal version of the cape of the Androgyne in the trump Art, which lies below the Priestess on the middle pillar. In this context, the arrow on her lap refers to Sagittarius, the zodiacal sign attributed to Art.

Crowley identifies the instrument on her lap as the bow of Artemis,[11] the Greek goddess attributed to this path. Artemis is the virgin goddess of the Moon and of hunters.

---

11. Crowley, *The Book of Thoth*, 73.

Lady Harris identifies the instrument as a sistrum,[12] a musical instrument that was originally a cult symbol of Hathor and was later associated with Isis. The sound of the sistrum was used to ward off malignant entities, and it attracted the blessings of the goddess.

Examination of the actual image in the trump shows that the instrument is a lyre, the instrument associated with Apollo, who was the brother of Artemis and a Sun god of Tiphareth. The path of Gimel connects Tiphareth and Kether, and it is the means by which the Adepts aspire to connect with the godhead.

On the lap of the Priestess, underneath the lyre, rests the Book of the Mysteries.[13] This book is symbolic of the esoteric knowledge possessed by the Priestess (as opposed to the exoteric instruction of the Hierophant). The path of Gimel is the only path on the Tree of Life that passes through the imaginary Sephira Daath (Hebrew for "knowledge"), which resides in the Abyss. The Book of the Mysteries is closed, as it is behind the veil of the Abyss, which conceals the supernal Sephiroth and their esoteric knowledge.

Inscribed on the base of the throne is an inverted crescent Moon, symbolic of the unconscious mind. The inverted crescent is also found in the Moon trump, where it appears at the top of the card. The position of the crescent Moon indicates the difference between the two lunar trumps. The Priestess illustrates the quality of initiated intuition that results from control of the unconscious mind, while the Moon shows the uncontrolled unconscious that generates darkness and illusion.

The Priestess sits between the pillars of Mercy and Severity. These are also the black and white pillars (Jachin and Boaz) found in the initiatory temples of Freemasonry and the Golden Dawn, where they represent the threshold over which the candidate must pass in order to gain assess to the mysteries of the temple. The pillars are silver, rayed sky blue, the color of the Moon in Atziluth.

Traditionally the veil of the Abyss is suspended between the white and black pillars, and the Priestess sits in front of the veil. In Crowley's trump, the Priestess sits behind the veil, and she spreads it out before her. Only the symbols in the foreground

---

12. Wasserman, James, *Instructions for Aleister Crowley's Thoth Tarot Deck* (Stamford, CT: U. S. Games Systems, Inc., 1983), 39.

13. Crowley, Aleister, *The Vision and the Voice with Commentary and Other Papers* (19th Aethyr) (Equinox 4:2) (York Beach, ME: Samuel Weiser, 1998), 105.

are in front of the veil, all indicative of manifestation below the Abyss. This suggests that you must penetrate the veil of the Abyss to gain access to the esoteric knowledge of the Priestess.

Two flowers bloom amidst the symbols in front of the veil. The first is a blossom of five petals surrounded by five larger petals. The second is a spiral-shaped flower of ten petals with a disk of seeds at its core. Ten is the number of Malkuth, manifestation. These flowers also reflect the energies of the pillars behind them; the concave petals of the first flower suggest the idea of form (Binah), while the spiral petals of the second flower are symbolic of force (Chokmah). The flowers are salmon and yellow, Tiphareth in Briah and Yetzirah, reflecting that this path connects to Tiphareth.

Below the flowers are the green pinecone of Bacchus and the grapes of Dionysus. Both are gods attributed to Tiphareth, yet they are also associated with the creative potential of unity expressed in the Fool.

In the lower corners are four geometric forms, two on each side of the Priestess. As solids, they represent the idea of manifestation below the Abyss. At the bottom of the card stands a camel, the meaning of Gimel. Like the Priestess, the camel is white, the color of Kether and Spirit. It is her symbolic emissary that travels the desert of Abyss of the Tree of Life.

Interpretation

In a reading, the Priestess signifies purity of mind, body, or spirit—the state of purity that facilitates the qualities of intuition, understanding, and gnosis in many different spiritual and religious traditions. The Book of the Mysteries indicates esoteric knowledge, understood only by those who penetrate the Veil of the Abyss by the exercise of intuition, emotion, and other ways of connecting with the unconscious mind. This trump also symbolizes aspiration unto the higher—be it spiritual, ethical, or otherwise.

The Priestess reversed brings corruption of the pure and denial of the spiritual. There may be a conflict between spiritual principles and the material world, or the manipulation of spiritual beliefs for material gain. As solar symbols, the flowers, grapes, and pinecone suggest that you may be mistaking the desires of the ego for the intuition of the unconscious mind, corrupting or severing the connection with your Higher Self.

III. The Empress

Hebrew Letter
Daleth

Meaning
Door

Attribution
Venus

Path
14th

Connects
Chokmah and Binah

The Empress is a glyph of feminine and maternal power. She is the archetypal Mother, possessing the highest aspects of Venus and the Moon.

The Empress is shown in profile, facing her counterpart in the Emperor. Her crown is similar to the lunar Crown of Isis found in the Priestess card. The orb and cross are symbols of dominion; these symbols are also found in the Emperor. The Maltese cross represents the four elements in perfect balance. The orb is placed above the head of the Empress, the position of Kether in the microcosm of man, and the Sephira above the path of Daleth on the Tree of Life.

The Empress's dress is rose and green, colors of Venus. Her garment is decorated with bees and dominoes. Crowley attributes the bee to the yoni[14] and to Binah, the Supernal Mother. The bee is also a symbol of energy and industriousness.

The word *domino* is French in origin, describing a Christian priest's hood that was black on the outside and white on the inside, and also a style of mask featuring a black and white motif. The overall concept is that of black and white counterchanged, symbolizing duality: light and dark, male and female, and Chokmah and Binah. The dominoes are surrounded by spiral designs that form roselike patterns on her garment, suggesting that the energy that unites and balances these dualistic forces is love.

The girdle of the zodiac around her waist is a representation of Nuit, the omnipresent mother

---

14. Crowley, Aleister, *777 and Other Qabalistic Writings of Aleister Crowley* (York Beach, ME: Samuel Weiser, 1993), 89.

and lover. The girdle is the magickal weapon of Venus, a sym-   *Figure 2*
bol of beauty and attraction.

The Empress holds the lotus of Isis to her breast. The
flower is placed over the heart chakra, the wellspring of love
and friendship. The blue lotus is a symbol of Water and its
powers of fertility and creativity. It also represents the yoni,
the vehicle of manifestation, and thus bears four petals, the
number of Chesed.

Her arms are positioned to suggest the alchemical symbol for Salt (see figure 2).
The alchemical element of Salt is feminine, passive, solid and heavy. Like the Empress, Salt is the vehicle of manifestation.

The Empress sits between the waning and waxing Moons. The waning crescent
is placed lower than the waxing crescent, and the nimbus of the waning Moon is
smaller in diameter than the waxing Moon. The Empress faces the waxing Moon,
which is associated with the ideas of growth and fertility inherent in this trump.
Perched upon her throne are a sparrow and a dove, birds sacred to Venus. Behind her
is an arch or door, the meaning of Daleth when spelled out in full.

At the base of the throne is a white rose, a symbol of Venus. Flowing from this rose
is the Water of Universal Life, the life-energy of the Great Sea of Binah.[15] The water is
tinged green, another connection to Venus and fertility. Two fish swim in the stream
flowing from the rose, the fish being a feminine symbol on account of its shape.

The carpet is adorned with the fleur-de-lis, a symbol representing the union of
the lingam and the yoni. There are a total of three emblems, suggesting a link with
the womb of Binah. There are many theories on the original symbolism of the fleur-
de-lis, but it most likely represents a stylized water lily or lotus. The central fleur-de-
lis is sky blue, the color of Venus in Briah.

The alchemical import of this card is revealed in the symbols of the shield and
the pelican.

The shield represents the White Tincture, the purified Salt analogous with silver
and the Moon. The shield is adorned with a white two-headed eagle, which is a symbol
of the gluten, the feminine sexual fluids of lubrication and ejaculation. Behind the
heads of the eagle is a waxing crescent Moon, symbolic of the lunar force embodied

---

15.   Venus is connected with the waters of Binah in the Star.

in the White Queen of the Lovers. The background is a mixture of green (Venus) and white (Spirit). The symbol of Venus is hidden in the design of the shield, formed by the nimbus of the lunar disk and the mid-torso, legs, and tail of the eagle.

The pelican feeding its young with its own blood is a common symbol of Christ and Christian virtue. It is an icon of maternal sacrifice, and therefore it is a symbol of the Aeon of Osiris. To confirm this connection, the pelican on this trump has twenty-four feathers to link it with the 24th path of the Death card and the figure of Osiris. The pelican is placed under the waning Moon and the shield stands under the waxing Moon, signifying the fading influence of the Old Aeon and the growing influence of the New Aeon.

The Empress, the shield, and the pelican symbolize a basic yet important alchemical process. The Empress represents the alchemical element of Salt. This Salt is separated into the White Tincture, represented by the shield, and the dross or impurities, signified by the pelican. The influence of the Old Aeon has been removed, particularly the ideas of sacrifice and the dying god, and especially those elements which demonize the feminine through subjugation and patriarchal dogma. These impurities are purged, and that which remains is the refined Salt of the New Aeon.

The catalyst in this separation is possibly antimony; the orb surmounted by the cross is also a symbol for antimony, a metal used in alchemy to remove impurities in the body that cause disease and the impurities in metals in order to transmute them into gold.

Interpretation

In a reading, the Empress indicates emotional well-being and satisfaction. Her garments and the shield signify the qualities of Venus: love, attraction, beauty, and pleasure. As the archetypal Mother, the Empress symbolizes maternal instincts, empathy, and nurturing behavior. Fertility, growth, and creativity are also aspects of this trump.

When the Empress is reversed, the qualities of Venus degrade into vanity, hedonism, and sexual or emotional manipulation. The pelican signifies maternal sacrifice and the subjection of women to traditional societal and familial roles. The reversed trump also indicates barrenness, decrease, and emotional pain.

The Emperor is a glyph of paternal and masculine power. He is the archetypal Father, associated with the qualities of the Sun, Mars, and Aries.

The Emperor is shown in profile and crowned. He resembles the Ancient of Days, an icon of Kether, the ultimate source of the Emperor's power and authority. His beard is a symbol of paternal power and maturity.

His golden crown is a symbol of the Sun, which rises behind him. This symbolism concurs with the traditional title of this card from *Book T*: "The Sun of the Morning, Chief among the Mighty."[16] The Sun is exalted in the sign of Aries, and Aries represents the renewal of solar energy in the yearly cycle.

The solar crown has four points and is adorned with jewels having four facets, indicating the authority associated with Jupiter, another paternal ruler. The Emperor resembles the Magickal Image of Chesed, a mighty king crowned and throned. The orb and scepter are also symbols associated with Chesed.

The Emperor holds a scepter crowned with a ram's head in his right hand. The rams in this card are symbols of Aries. This trump is mostly painted in the red colors of Mars, the ruler of Aries. He holds this scepter as if to absorb the light streaming down from the upper right of the card. This light represents the influence of Chokmah, the archetypal Father.

IV. The Emperor

Hebrew Letter
Tzaddi

Meaning
Fish hook

Attribution
Aries

Path
15th

Connects
Netzach and Yesod

---

16. Regardie, Israel, *The Golden Dawn*, 6th ed., (St. Paul, MN: Llewellyn, 1995), 542.

Figure 3

In his left hand, he cradles an orb surmounted with a Maltese cross, a symbol of dominion. The Emperor holds the orb and cross over his navel chakra, the center of procreative sexual energy and sexual pleasure—characteristics associated with the Moon (Yesod) and Venus (Netzach) respectively.

The Emperor's garment is embroidered with bees, symbols of energy and industriousness. The bee is associated with the fertilization process of the flower. The hive structure of bees is highly organized, suggesting the ideas of order and government. The other design found on the Emperor's garment is a series of looping lines that terminate in arrowheads, which emphasize the ideas of energy and activity associated with this trump.

The arms and legs of the Emperor form a cross surmounted by a triangle, the alchemical symbol for Sulfur (see figure 3). Sulfur is masculine, active, volatile, and fiery in nature. Each arm of his throne is adorned with a star of sixteen points, the atomic number of Sulfur. Sixteen is also the gematria of *Chach*, hook, which is the meaning of Tzaddi.

On the carpet below his feet is the fleur-de-lis. The symbol is associated with the French monarchy, and as a symbol of rulership is appropriate to this card. It also represents the union of the lingam and the yoni as discussed in the section on the Empress.

The alchemical import of the Emperor is revealed in the symbols of the shield and the Lamb and Flag.

The Emperor's shield represents the Red Tincture, the purified Sulfur analogous with gold and the Sun. The golden eagle with two heads has its origin in heraldry, where it is a symbol of imperial power. The eagle's fiery feathers connect it with the phoenix, a symbol of regenerative fire. The solar disk behind the eagle identifies this trump with gold and the Red King found in the Lovers.

The Lamb and Flag is a Christian symbol known as *Agnus Dei*, Latin for "Lamb of God." The lamb was often the preferred blood sacrifice in the Old Testament.[17] Christians identify the Lamb and Flag with Jesus Christ, who was sacrificed to atone for mankind's sins. As a Christian symbol of sacrifice, the Lamb and Flag is associ-

---

17. Note that the gematria of *dam*, Hebrew for blood, and *taleh*, lamb, both enumerate to forty-four.

ated with the Aeon of Osiris. The lamb is weak and docile, while the ram of Aries is strong and aggressive.

The same alchemical process described in the Empress also takes place in this trump. The Emperor represents Sulfur, which is refined into the Red Tincture. The Old Aeon/Christian idea of sacrifice symbolized by the Lamb and Flag has been removed and discarded. Thus, the light from above shines upon the shield, leaving the Lamb and Flag in darkness.

The catalyst in this process is antimony, symbolized by the orb and cross. The process of calcination may also be involved: Aries is associated with the alchemical process of calcination, the reduction and purification of the base metal through the application of intense heat.

Interpretation

The primary interpretations of the Emperor in a reading are concerned with power and control, either over other people or over yourself. The crown, scepter, and orb are symbols of authority, leadership, and governance, and therefore this trump indicates structure in society and in personal life. As the archetypal Father, the Emperor signifies paternal instincts and the enforcement of rules and regulations.

When this trump is reversed, the negative characteristics of power are present. The Emperor becomes an instigator of war, aggression, cruelty, and violence. Oppressive government and strict rules may stifle freedom and progress. Alternatively, the influence of the Lamb and Flag may come to bear, signifying weakness and submission. This implies an inability to enforce rules or bring structure to a situation.

V. The Hierophant

Hebrew Letter
Vau

Meaning
Nail

Attribution
Taurus

Path
16th

Connects
Chokmah and Chesed

The Hierophant is a glyph of the three Thelemic Aeons. As the initiator of the Mysteries, he receives the force and wisdom of Chokmah and organizes and distributes it unto Chesed.

The design of this trump resembles the Magickal Image of Chesed, a mighty king crowned and throned. The Hierophant is bearded, symbolic of maturity and paternal power. In this respect, he also resembles the Magickal Image of Chokmah, a mature, bearded man.

The Hierophant wears the Crown of Osiris, reflecting his connection with Osiris in the initiation rituals of the Golden Dawn. As the Master of the Hall in the Golden Dawn rituals, the Hierophant conducts the initiation of the candidate and instructs him in the mysteries of the temple. His throne is in the East, the place of the rising Sun, and he is the link between the members of the Outer Order and the Adepts of the Inner Order of the Golden Dawn.

The crown and the robe of the Hierophant are red-orange, Taurus in Atziluth. He is enthroned upon the bull of Taurus, the Kerub of Earth, which is the foundation upon which the Great Work is accomplished. Note that Osiris is also associated with the bull-god Apis of Memphis. Flanking the Hierophant are elephants, which are associated with Taurus as beasts of burden.

With his left hand, the Hierophant makes the sign of esotericism and blessing. In his right hand, the Hierophant holds a wand crowned with three interlocking rings, a symbol of the three Thelemic

26

Aeons of Isis, Osiris, and Horus.[18] The three figures in this card also represent the three Aeons; the Hierophant is Osiris, the woman is Isis, and the child is Horus.

Standing in front of the Hierophant is a woman holding a large sword, which illustrates a verse from *The Book of the Law*: "Let the woman be girt with a sword before me: let blood flow to my name" (AL III:11). The general idea is that women are equal and worthy warriors of Thelema, that "every man and every woman is a star" (AL I:3).

The sword also represents the phallus, and thus she is the Woman Satisfied of the trump Adjustment. She holds the sword between her thighs, and where the sword crosses her womb, a ray of light brings forth the child Horus. This woman therefore also represents Isis, the wife of Osiris and the mother of Horus. The lunar crescent that she bears links her with the Priestess, which shows Isis throned. The crescent is also the bow of Artemis the huntress.

Imposed upon the image of the Hierophant is a hexagram. Within the hexagram is an inverted pentagram, and within the inverted pentagram is an upright pentagram. These symbols signify the unification of the macrocosm (hexagram) with the microcosm (pentagrams).

Dancing within the upright pentagram is the child Horus. While the other figures in this trump appear solemn and rigid, Horus is active and playful. Horus is a solar deity, and he dances over the solar plexus of the Hierophant. Horus is also the Son, the Vau of Tetragrammaton.

This dynamic nature of Horus is further indicated by the sandal strap on his right foot, the symbol of the fifth Power of the Sphinx, to Go. The concept of the four Powers of the Sphinx (to Know, to Will, to Dare, and to Keep Silent) finds its origin in the works of Eliphas Lévi, and they correspond with the four elements. Crowley added a fifth Power of the Sphinx to correspond with the element of Spirit.

Behind the Hierophant is an oriel, a window with a rose-shaped bracket. The white light shining through the oriel is the brilliance of the Supernals, the macrocosmic knowledge transmitted through the Hierophant. The light doubles as a nimbus or a halo, a characteristic of the enlightened. The rose is a symbol of Venus, the ruler of Taurus. In contrast, the dove and the serpent that encircle the oriel are symbols associated with the Tower and Mars in *The Book of the Law* (see AL I:57.) The bracket is

---

18. Crowley, *The Book of Thoth*, 79–80.

scarlet, Mars in Atziluth. The nails are nine in number to indicate Yesod (the womb of the Tree of Life) and the Moon, which is exalted in Taurus. The window is Hé, which is the Star, an image of Nuit, the archetypal Mother; in this context, the oriel is a window into the macrocosmic universe.

In the corners of the card are the four Kerubim, who represent the four Powers of the Sphinx. They appear as hollow masks, inert and lifeless, for the Hierophant can only instruct the candidate of their nature and use; it is by experience alone that these doctrines may be brought to life.[19]

Interpretation

The Hierophant is an initiating priest and enlightened teacher, and in a reading indicates instruction and exoteric knowledge. If exercised, the teachings of the Hierophant may lead to esoteric knowledge, an intuitive understanding that is signified by the Priestess standing before him. The child reminds us that learning is an active, enjoyable, and satisfying process, as young children are often eager to learn and experience new things. Endurance, patience, and physical labor are also characteristics of this card, qualities associated with the bull of Taurus.

The Hierophant reversed signifies false knowledge and mistaken beliefs that interfere with the resolution of an issue in the reading. Rigid religious or spiritual dogma that stifles the development and learning of the individual may also be involved. It often shows a person unwilling to learn or apply what has been learned. Like the kerubic masks in the corners of this trump, the mere accumulation of knowledge is a hollow and lifeless pursuit if it is not put into practice. The negative traits of Taurus also creep in: laziness, inertia, and resistance to change.

---

19. The Kerubim also appear in the last trump of the major arcana, the Universe, where they are portrayed as living creatures.

The Lovers is a glyph of analysis. It illustrates the alchemical process of *solve*, where the First Matter (the impure metal or body) is divided into its essential parts and purified in preparation for reintegration (*coagula*) in Art.

At the center of the card stands the Hermit from the Hermit trump, who officiates over the Hermetic Marriage of the Black King and White Queen. The Hermit represents Yod, the creative power, and Virgo, potential fertility and virility. The scroll about his arms is the Logos of Mercury, the word of creation and unification, and the Hermit stands in the Sign of the Enterer to direct this creative force. Mercury is the Magus, the messenger of Kether, and the white light behind the Hermit's head is the blessing of the Crown. His robe is purple, Mercury in Briah.

The Hermit represents alchemical Mercury, the agent of transformation that unites Sulfur and Salt. The King and Queen who stand before the Hermit wear the same crowns as the figures in the Emperor and the Empress trumps, identifying them with the Red and White Tinctures, the purified Sulfur and Salt.

The King's crown is gold, signifying the Sun, and the Queen's crown is silver, signifying the Moon. This alludes to the marriage of the Sun and the Moon, a common theme in alchemical symbolism. The King wears a five-pointed crown, the number of Geburah, while the crown of the Queen is adorned with the Orb and Cross, a symbol of Chesed. The King's robe is embroidered with serpents coiled into lemniscates to signify the eternal cycle of life, death and rebirth, while the bees embroidered upon the Queen's robe are symbols of fertility.

VI. The Lovers

Hebrew Letter
Zayin

Meaning
Sword

Attribution
Gemini

Path
17th

Connects
Binah and Tiphareth

A lion and eagle sit behind the King and Queen. The lion (as Leo) is a symbol of elemental Fire, and the eagle (as Scorpio) is a symbol of Water. The lion's tail rises up from
his loins like an erect phallus. The lion has five kinks in his tail, while the eagle has four
tail feathers, a reflection of the Geburah-Chesed polarity expressed in the crowns.

The King holds the Sacred Lance, representative of the phallus, and the Queen
holds the Holy Grail, a symbol of the womb. The lance and grail are the primary
magickal tools of the priest and priestess in the Gnostic Mass, an enactment of the
Hermetic Marriage. The cup is adorned with the dove of Venus, the attribution of
the Empress. The five white rays emanating from the cup indicate the fifth element
of Spirit, and the dove is also a symbol of Spirit.

A black child and a white child assist the King and Queen. The twins represent
Gemini, the zodiacal sign attributed to this trump. They are the only complementary opposites in this card that are counterchanged, the white child standing with the
Black King and the black child next to the White Queen. The white nimbus around
the twins and the fact that they stand upon the wings of the Orphic Egg suggests
that they represent the spirit or potential of the Orphic Egg, the symbolic product of
the union of the King and Queen. Thus the twins represent the forthcoming union
and integration of opposites depicted on Art. These twins evolved from the infants
in the Fool, and they will be fully emancipated in the Sun.

The twins are also the solar twins Vau Hé, Ra-Hoor-Khuit, and Heru-Pa-Kraat.
The solar twins represent strength and silence, characteristics reflected in the black
club and white roses. The club is a weapon and is therefore is a symbol of Mars and
Geburah, while the roses are four in number, indicating Chesed.

The serpent coiled around the egg is the Orphic Egg that contains the universe,
according to Greek mythology. The Egg is a symbol of the ideal or potential of the
Hermetic Marriage, as the Egg is painted in the colors of the supernal Sephiroth:
white, gray, and black. It has crimson wings, the color of Binah in Atziluth. The serpent is purple, the color of Mercury in Briah; Mercury is associated with Chokmah
as the "higher octave" of Mercury. The Orphic Egg also appears in the Hermit, but
on that trump the colors of the Egg and serpent refer to Netzach and Hod. The Hermit shows the Orphic Egg in a more manifest state.

The Orphic Egg is the product of the union of the King and Queen. This union
is also symbolized by the orange "cone" above the Egg where the red and yellow
robes overlap. Orange is the color of Mercury in Atziluth. This overlap bears the

serpent and the bee, the same symbols combined on the robe of the Androgyne in the Art card.

The lion, eagle, and Orphic Egg rest upon a bow concealed at the bottom of the card. The lance doubles as an arrow for this bow. This is another reference to the Art trump, whose attribution is Sagittarius the Archer.

The figure hovering above the Hermit is Eros, the Roman god of love. Thelema is written upon his quiver, and the arrow is a symbol of directed will. He represents love and will, the two principles necessary for the Hermetic Marriage to take place. While "love is the law, love under will" (AL I:57), there is also the understanding that "there is no bond that can unite the divided but love: all else is a curse" (AL I:41).

Flanking Eros at the top of the trump are the figures of Eve and Lilith. Eve and Lilith represent the duality of Binah, the Sephira from which this path originates. Eve is Aima, the bright and fertile Mother, while Lilith is Ama, the dark and sterile Mother. In Hebrew, the difference between these two names of Binah is the letter Yod, symbolic of fertility and represented by the Hermit between them.

Eve, Lilith, and Eros are symbols from the traditional design of this card.[20] The old Lovers trump indicated a choice or decision, stressing the cleaving action of the sword (Zayin) of the intellect. Crowley has pushed them to the top of the card, out of the way of the new interpretation that is not simple choice but full analysis.

The background of the trump is a symbolic representation of this path on the Tree of Life. Eve and Lilith stand at the top of two black pillars, representative of Binah as the Gate of Life and Death. Beyond the pillars is an arch of swords that leads to the light of Kether. The archway is painted in solar hues to indicate the harmonious influence of Tiphareth.

Interpretation

In a reading, the Lovers signifies analysis, carefully looking at all aspects of a situation before making a conclusion. It indicates the careful planning involved in important decisions, such as business ventures or marriage. The Hermit unites the King and Queen, and thus symbolizes mediation between opposing sides in a dispute and reconciliation in disagreements.

---

20. A good example of this arrangement can be found in the Lovers trump of the Tarot of Marseilles.

The Lovers reversed indicates the lack of analysis of a situation, and it may signify an impulsive or uninformed decision. Overanalysis of a situation may also be indicated, which may keep you from making a decision. The sword is an instrument of division, and it symbolizes quarrels, disagreements, and arguments.

The Chariot is a glyph of the Adept, who crosses the Abyss on the path of Cheth.

The crest on the Adept's helmet is the crab of Cancer, the zodiacal sign attributed to this card. The Adept's armor is amber, the color of Cancer in Atziluth, and it alludes to the Cancerian quality of protection. His armor is adorned with ten stars, attributed to the world of Assiah.[21] The number ten and Assiah are associated with Malkuth, the Bride or Inferior Mother. These star-studs are sapphires, and the star sapphire is attributed to Binah, the Supernal Mother. This symbolism reflects the link between the origin of form in Binah and its final manifestation on the material plane of Malkuth.

The body and the face reveal a great deal about the personality of the individual; the Adept is completely covered with armor, and thus no such judgments can be made. This represents the destruction of the personality (ego) that the Adept must attain in order to successfully traverse the Abyss.

The Adept sits cross-legged, as if deep in meditation. He sits upon a silvery lunar crescent, which is symbolic of the unconscious mind dominated and harnessed by the Adept. It also signifies the rulership of Cancer by the Moon. He is covered with a white cloak, symbolic of inner purity. The red cloak worn over it symbolizes his passion. These are the same vestments worn by the Priest in the Gnostic Mass.

The wheels of the chariot are scarlet, the color of Geburah in Briah. Red is also a color of Mars, which is exalted in Cancer. Geburah provides the

---

21. Crowley, *The Book of Thoth*, 85.

VII. The Chariot

Hebrew Letter
Cheth

Meaning
Fence

Attribution
Cancer

Path
18th

Connects
Binah and Geburah

energy and impetus to propel the chariot across the Abyss to Binah. The posts or pillars that hold up the canopy of the chariot are maroon, the color of Cancer in Briah. The pillars are aligned with the four Sphinxes sitting in front of the chariot. The front pillars extend down to the bull and the lion-headed Sphinxes, while the back pillars reach down to the eagle and man-headed Sphinxes.[22] The pillars, like the path of Cheth, span the Abyss between Geburah (chariot) and Binah (canopy). This indicates that proper understanding and practice of the four Powers of the Sphinx has prepared the Adept to cross the Abyss. It is the Powers of the Sphinx that drive the chariot. They are not bridled and reined to the Adept; they are integral parts of the Adept.

Written along the edge of the canopy of the chariot is the word ABRACADABRA, a curious variant of ABRAHADABRA. Crowley has substituted the Hebrew letter Cheth for Hé to emphasize the connection between the letter and the word of the Aeon.[23] Cheth spelled in full adds up to 418, the numeration of ABRAHADABRA, the Word of the Aeon of Horus.

ABRAHADABRA has eleven letters, the number of magick. It can be divided into five vowels and six consonants, and thus shows the union of man (the pentagram) and God (the hexagram), the Great Work accomplished. On the Tree of Life, the formula ABRAHADABRA is attributed to Tiphareth, where the initial union of Man and God takes place in the achievement of the knowledge and conversation of the Higher Self.

The Adept travels a road made of twenty-one square bricks. Twenty-one is the value of Eheieh, a god-name of Kether, which is the ultimate destination of the Adept. The chariot travels on the road to the godhead.

The chariot emerges from the waters of the Great Sea of Binah. The ripples on the surface of the sea emanate from the most important feature of this card, the Holy Grail. The Grail is made of pure amethyst, the stone attributed to Jupiter. The rim of the cup is violet, Jupiter in Atziluth, and the bowl is blue, Jupiter in Briah. The

---

22. This concept is also found in (and may have originated from) Papus's *Tarot of the Bohemians* (London: Senate, 1994), 135: "This symbol reproduces the 1st and 21st arcana in another order of ideas. The four columns represent the four animals of the 21st arcanum, and the four symbols of the 1st arcanum, symbols of the *quaternary* in all its acceptations."

23. Note that while the Hebrew letter Cheth is normally pronounced hard (as in *change*), it may also be pronounced soft (as in *hang*).

handles of the grail are composed of four spirals, the number of Chesed (Jupiter) and the last Sephira that must be mastered before crossing the Abyss.

Six rays emanate from the center of the Grail, representing the influence of Tiphareth. The red sphere with the point in the center forms the sigil of the Sun, and the Sun reaches the pinnacle of its power and potency when it enters Cancer at the Summer Solstice. The red blood in the Grail is semen,[24] the seed within the womb, signifying the accomplishment of the Great Work.

Interpretation

In a reading, the Chariot signifies a significant victory or triumph over adversity. The Sphinxes and the other attributes of the Adept in this card stress that proper preparation is necessary for victory to be achieved. Self-control over passions (symbolized by the red cloak and wheels), unconscious desires (the lunar crescent), and the ego are also indicated. As a vehicle, the chariot symbolizes action, moving forward with plans or taking advantage of opportunities. The protective qualities of Cancer are also present, represented by the armor, helm, and crest of the Adept.

The Chariot reversed indicates failure and defeat, often from failure to take action or from being unprepared. You may be overprotective or too cautious to move forward and meet new challenges. A lack of self-control may lead to violence or self-destructive behaviors. This may also signify a compulsion to control others to make up for a lack of self-control.

---

24. See the trump Art.

VIII.
Adjustment

Hebrew Letter
Lamed

Meaning
Ox-goad

Attribution
Libra

Path
22nd

Connects
Geburah and Tiphareth

Adjustment is a glyph of equilibrium and balance. It illustrates the process by which the Daughter of the Tetragrammaton (the Final Hé) matures into the Mother (the Primal Hé).

Crowley has changed the title of this trump from *Justice* to *Adjustment* to reflect that maintaining equilibrium is an active process. Gone is the static figure of Justice, seated and blindfolded; this trump recognizes the aphorism that "change is stability."

Justice wears a mask with tiny arched eyeholes, and leggings printed with a crisscross diamond pattern, symbols associated with Harlequin, the archetypal fool of the Italian commedia dell'arte. The Harlequin's attributes allude to the link between Adjustment and the Fool in the Thelemic formula AL (Aleph-Lamed). *AL* means "God" in Hebrew, and the letters can be reversed to spell *LA*, Hebrew for "not." These formulae express the 0=2 equation as LA (not, nothing) and AL (God, all, the duality of manifestation). Opposing forces, when properly balanced, will cancel each other out. The letters *AL* are also linked by their meanings, as Aleph is an ox and Lamed is the ox-goad that is used to keep the ox moving in the proper direction.

Justice is crowned with the blue ostrich feathers of Maat, the Egyptian goddess of justice. Maat is the personification of an exalted concept of morality, truth, and order, both in the microcosm and in the macrocosm. The Egyptian word *maat* may be translated not only as "justice" but also as "truth," "right," and even "that which is straight." Maat is that which brings and maintains order in the universe.

Justice also corresponds with Thmaist, the god-form of the Hegemon in the Neophyte Ceremony of the Golden Dawn. It is the Hegemon who adjusts and balances the energies of the Ceremony (especially the cup-bearing Stolistes and the censer-bearing Dadouchos), and whose station in the temple is between the black and white pillars of Severity and Mercy.

The figure of Justice is balanced on the point of the Great Sword of the Magician.[25] The design of the Great Sword carefully balances masculine and feminine symbolism to reflect the equal influence of the Father (Yod) and the Mother (Primal Hé) in the manifestation of the Son (Vau) and the Daughter (Final Hé). The Great Sword of the Magician is also a symbol of the True Will, and Thelema is inscribed on the blade.

The sword is the weapon of Geburah as a symbol of judgment and punishment. The traditional image of the trump Justice, with scales in one hand and the sword in the other, suggests the process of judgment is forthcoming or taking place. In contrast, the image of Adjustment, in which the woman, scales, and sword are balanced, indicates that judgment has already occurred, and that which had created an imbalance has been cut away by the sword.

The sword is also a phallus, held between the thighs of Justice to symbolize the sexual act. It is in this manner that the Daughter becomes the Mother. She is the Woman Satisfied.

Suspended from her crown are balances or spheres equating the Alpha and the Omega, the beginning and the end. The balances and chains are black to show the influence of Saturn, the planet exalted in Libra. Saturn indicates the element of time, the context of all change. The spheres are also testicles, the complement of the phallic sword.

The throne behind Justice is perfectly balanced between blue and green spheres. In the court cards of the tarot, only the Queens are enthroned. The Princess (Final Hé) may only assume the throne of the Queen (Primal Hé) when she matures into a woman. As the Woman Satisfied, Justice has earned the right to assume the throne of equilibrium.

---

25. For a description of the Great Sword of the Magician, see Crowley, Aleister, *Liber ABA, Book 4, parts I–IV* (York Beach, ME: Samuel Weiser, 2000), 87. The Great Sword of the Magician also appears in the Ace of Swords.

The spheres in this trump are perfectly counterchanged both horizontally and vertically. They are blue and green, the colors of this path in Atziluth and Briah, and thus symbolize the balance of masculine and feminine energies. The sphere that Justice balances on is both blue and green; it is completely equilibrated.

The trump is framed with curtains adorned with a diamond pattern, and the curtains form a large diamond around the figure of Justice. The diamond is a symbol of Kether that first appears in the Fool, and thus it alludes to the connection between the Fool and Adjustment and the formula AL. The curtain is also the hymen, which is broken when the Daughter becomes the Mother.

Interpretation

The primary interpretations of Adjustment in a reading are obvious: equilibrium, balance, and adjustment. The sword and scales indicate judgment and justice favorable to the querent, particularly in legal matters. Truth and order are symbolized by the feathers of Maat, and thus it is advisable to seek or tell the truth in the situation concerned. The appearance of Adjustment may also signify a woman or a man coming to maturity, or anyone becoming or being responsible for his own balance, judgment, or truth.

Adjustment reversed indicates imbalance and falsehood. The conservative influence of Saturn implies a resistance to change or adjustment. It may also signify a delay in receiving justice, or a judgment against the querent. Finally, the reversed trump may symbolize a lack of responsibility or maturity.

The Hermit is a glyph of potential yet unmanifested life in the form of the sperm, the creative but virgin seed symbolized by Yod and Virgo.

The Hermit stands in a field of ripened wheat, and Virgo is the sign of the harvest. The cloak of the Hermit is plum, the color of Virgo in Atziluth. His beard and hair are white with age, and his face is concealed. These are symbolic characteristics of Kether, known by the titles *the White Head, the Ancient of Days*, and *the Concealed of the Concealed*. Kether is the ultimate source of the creative power symbolized in this trump.

The Hermit holds a lamp containing the Sun. It is the same Sun found in the Fool, and in both trumps the Sun is placed over the genitals as a glyph of creative light. In this trump, the Sun is composed of eight straight and eight wavy rays, suggesting a relationship with Mercury, the planet ruled by Virgo. The lamp has eight sides, another link to Hod and Mercury.

The Hermit adores the Orphic Egg, which first appears in the Lovers. The green tint of the egg is the color of Venus and Netzach, the complement of Mercury (the serpent) and Hod. This is in turn a reflection of the dynamic relationship between Binah and Chokmah, for the Egg is a form that contains the universe, and the Mercurial serpent represents force.

At the feet of the Hermit is the Serpent Wand, which also resembles a sperm. The head of the wand is cleverly drawn to show both the head of a serpent and a fetus curled up in the fetal position. The fetus symbolizes the potential of the sperm, and the four-pointed star on the top of its head represents the seed of the four elements that make up all manifest life.

IX. The Hermit

Hebrew Letter
Yod

Meaning
Hand

Attribution
Virgo

Path
20th

Connects
Chesed and Tiphareth

Following the Hermit is the three-headed dog Cerberus, the guardian of the ada-mantine gates of Tartarus in Greek mythology. In relation to Cerberus, the Hermit takes on Mercury's role of psychopomp, bearing the light that guides souls through the underworld. He has tamed Cerberus, signifying that he has overcome the powers of death.

There is a deeper symbolism connected with Cerberus revealed in Crowley's *Liber Jugorum*:

> *1. Three are the Beasts wherewith thou must plough the Field; the Uni-corn, the Horse, and the Ox. And these shalt thou yoke in a triple yoke that is governed by One Whip.*
>
> *2. Now these Beasts run wildly upon the earth and are not easily obedient to the Man.*
>
> *3. Nothing shall be said here of Cereberus, the great Beast of Hell that is every one of these and all of these, even as Athanasius hath foreshadowed. For this matter is not of Tiphareth without, but Tiphareth within.*[26]

Further on in *Liber Jugorum*, Crowley ascribes human attributes to each of the three beasts and then presents exercises through which one may become the master of each of these attributes. The unicorn is speech, the horse is action, and the ox is thought. As defined in the quote above, Cerberus represents the attributes of all three beasts (three heads, three beasts).

The Hermit has tamed Cerberus, signifying that he has full control over his fac-ulties of speech, action, and thought. The three heads of Cerberus in this trump reflect the qualities of these attributes. The first head has his mouth open and rep-resents speech. The last head is turned to look behind Cerberus and signifies action. The central head, held higher than the other two, is firm and meditative in his de-meanor and represents thought.

There are two rays of light in the top half of the card that do not emanate from the lamp. These two rays are outlined in white, while the rays of the lamp are out-lined in yellow. The white rays compose the hidden background of the trump; the triangular beam forms two sides of a pyramid, while the roughly horizontal beam of light below it is the horizon (see figure 4).

---

26. The full version of *Liber III vel Jugorum* can be found in Crowley's *Liber ABA*, 647.

The pyramid is symbolic of the phallus,[27] the means by which the sperm (the virgin seed) is transmitted. The sexual operation by which this takes place is shown symbolically in the Hermit, the rays of light from the lamp corresponding with the points of the pyramid of light.

Following the movement of the Hermit from right to left, the first ray of light illuminates the sperm in the lower left corner, the unrealized potential of life. The second ray of light is vertical, reaching down from the apex of the pyramid/phallus to illuminate the lamp of the Sun. It is representative of the erect and creative phallus, held by the hand. The third ray of light, pointing to the other end of the pyramid just in front of the figure of the Hermit, illuminates Cerberus, the guardian of the land of the dead, who symbolizes the "dead" phallus after ejaculation. The fourth and final ray points to the Orphic Egg, showing the sperm and egg conjoined; the egg has been fertilized, and a new life has been created. In the context of sex magick, the Orphic Egg also symbolizes the power of the orgasm united with the intent of the magician.

Figure 4

Interpretation

In a reading, the Hermit indicates illumination, symbolized by the lamp in the center of the card. The darkness is dispelled, and that which was hidden is revealed. This trump also signifies isolation: removing yourself from a situation in order to gain insight. It may be time to retire from a job or project and move on to something new.

The Hermit reversed signifies secrecy, concealing the facts, and obfuscating the truth. You may be isolating yourself from those who can help you, or exhibiting antisocial behavior. The reversed trump also indicates that it may be beneficial to be more social, to get out and interact with the world at large. It may be the time to break secrecy and expose projects or situations to the public.

---

27. Crowley, Aleister, *Magick Without Tears*, edited by Israel Regardie (Tempe, AZ: New Falcon, 1991), 12.

X. Fortune

Hebrew Letter
Kaph

Meaning
Fist

Attribution
Jupiter

Path
21st

Connects
Chesed and Netzach

Fortune is a glyph of the machinery of the universe expressed as the three alchemical principles spinning on a wheel.

The wheel has ten spokes and spins counter-clockwise, drawing in ten plumes of energy like a whirlpool. Ten is the number of Malkuth, the manifest universe governed by the action of the wheel. At the bottom of the wheel is a fist, the meaning of the word *Kaph*. It is symbolic of the hand of Fortunata or fate that spins the wheel. Six rays emanate from the fist, the number of Tiphareth, indicating that the force that moves the wheel is balanced.

There are three figures on the rim of the wheel: Hermanubis, Typhon, and the Sphinx. They correspond with the three alchemical principles of Mercury, Salt, and Sulfur.

Ascending the wheel is Hermanubis, who represents the alchemical principle of Mercury. Hermanubis is a composite form of Hermes and Anubis. Both gods functioned as psychopomps, guiding souls between the material and the spiritual worlds. Likewise, Mercury is the fluid element that mediates between Salt and Sulfur.

Plutarch insisted that Hermanubis was actually Heru-em-Anpu, or Horus as Anubis.[28] This form unifies light (Horus) and darkness (Anubis), and thus also performs the Mercurial function of the unification of opposing principles, as seen in the Lovers.

While Crowley identifies the figure ascending the wheel as Hermanubis, the actual figure in the card resembles the Cynocephalus Ape of the Ma-

---

28. Budge. *Gods of the Egyptians*, vol. 2, 265.

gus, Mercury. To confirm his association with Mercury, the Ape wears a coat of fifteen segments, the numeration of Hod.

Descending the wheel is Typhon, who represents the alchemical principle of Salt. The symbol for Salt appears on his head behind his eye to confirm this attribution.

According to Greek myth, Typhon was a Titan, the youngest son of Gaia (the Earth) and Tartarus (the underworld). Typhon was a terrifying and enormous monster, and his most prominent attribute was that he was nothing but coiled serpents below the waist. Thus in the trump his serpentine body is coiled around the rim of the wheel.

Typhon attacked Olympus, seeking revenge for the defeat and death of his brothers, the Giants and the Titans. After a series of battles with Zeus (including one conflict in which Zeus was defeated, then rescued by Hermes and Pan), Typhon was finally overcome by Zeus's thunderbolts and buried when Zeus hurled Mount Aetna upon him. Elements of this myth are reflected in the symbolism of this trump. Zeus is Jupiter, and his thunderbolts descend from the sky. Typhon is struck and falls from the wheel, to be crushed under it as he was crushed under Mount Aetna.

Typhon is also associated with Set, the Egyptian god of storms and darkness. Set was the slayer of Osiris, and in this trump he is shown separating the Ankh of Life from the Crook of Osiris.

The Sphinx sitting atop the wheel represents the alchemical principle of Sulfur. She has the head of a woman and the body of a lion, symbolic of the balance of male and female forces. The Sphinx represents the union of Babalon (the woman) and the Beast (the lion) that is expressed in the trump Lust. She holds a sword between her paws, a symbol of martial and masculine energy associated with the Emperor, who is associated with Sulfur.

In the background, behind the wheel, is an equilateral triangle. This shape expresses the balance of the three alchemical principles upon the rim of the wheel. The axle of the wheel is placed in the uppermost point of the triangle to form the Eye in the Triangle, a symbol of spiritual enlightenment. Above the wheel is a circle of stars, an abstract representation of Nuit. In this context, the triangle represents Hadit, who is "the axle of the wheel" (AL II:7). Around the rim of the circle are five-pointed stars. Five is the number of man, just as the pentagram is the symbol of the microcosm. The idea is that "every man and every woman is a star" (AL I:3). The stars are distorted to reflect that every person is unique.

At the center of the circle is a ten-pointed star, a reflection of the star at the center of the wheel. This relationship illustrates the Hermetic axiom "That which is above is as that which is below."

Interpretation

In a reading, Fortune indicates a favorable development in situations in which an element of chance is involved and the outcome is uncertain. The Sphinx at the top of the wheel symbolizes taking control of your fate or destiny and acting upon un-expected opportunities as they arise. The rising figure of Hermanubis signifies the ability to adapt to changing circumstances. In all cases, it is advisable to look at the bigger picture, the full implications of your actions in the universe.

When Fortune is reversed, Typhon ascends to the top of the wheel, bringing bad luck and dark times. You may be at the mercy of circumstances beyond your control. It is only by individual effort that you will be able to overcome the forces that work against you.

Lust is a glyph of sexual and magickal power, showing Babalon and the Beast conjoined in sexual union.

The traditional design of this card shows a woman holding open the jaws of a lion, symbolic of the conscious will controlling the animal passions and desires. This concept manifests in Lust as Babalon dominating the lion-beast. In Lust, the conscious will not only controls the animal passions but also unites with them.

Crowley's trump design corresponds with the description of Babalon and the Beast presented in the Book of Revelation:

> So he carried me away in the spirit into the wilderness: and I saw a woman sit upon a scarlet colored beast, full of names of blasphemy, having seven heads and ten horns.
>
> And the woman was arrayed in purple and scarlet color, and decked with gold and precious stones and pearls, having a golden cup in her hand full of abominations and filthiness of her fornication.[29]

The seven heads of the Beast represent the seven chakras. Babalon has activated the chakras of the Beast and absorbed the energy into her womb, the Holy Grail. Above her rears the Kundalini serpent, awakened and aroused by sexual union. Note that

XI. Lust

Hebrew Letter
Teth

Meaning
Snake

Attribution
Leo

Path
19th

Connects
Chesed and Geburah

---

29. Revelation 17:3–4.

Babalon is gazing at the lion-serpent, symbolic of the phallus, while the Beast faces the Holy Grail, the womb.

Chapter 49 of *The Book of Lies* identifies the seven heads of the Beast as an angel, a saint, a poet, an adulterous woman, a man of valor, a satyr, and a lion-serpent.[30] The seven heads represent different aspects of Aleister Crowley, who associated himself with the Beast. Crowley was a poet and a man of valor; the adulterous woman and the satyr refer to his sexual habits, the adulterous woman even suggestive of his bisexuality; and Crowley made himself a saint in the Gnostic Catholic Church. The first and last heads are explained in the commentary on Chapter 49: "the word 'angel' may refer to his mission, and the word 'lion-serpent' to the sigil of his ascending decan."[31] Crowley's rising sign is Leo.

The tail of the Beast is a lion-serpent, a symbol that combines the lion of Leo with the serpent, the meaning of Teth spelled out in full. The lion-serpent has a nimbus of thirteen rays, the number of the Hebrew words *achad* (unity) and *ahbah* (love). This relationship is explained by *The Book of the Law*: "There is no bond that can unite the divided but love: all else is a curse" (AL I:41). The lion-serpent also appears in the Tower card, where it is a symbol of the dawning Aeon of Horus.

Babalon sits naked upon the Beast, her head thrown back in the ecstasy of orgasm. She holds up the Holy Grail, which contains the sacrament of the sexual act. The sacrament is the semen and gluten commingled, the distillation of the Sun and the Moon that occurs in the internal ferment of the womb.

Above the horizon dawns the light of a new life. Ten rays of light bring order to the ten Sephiroth, which represent Adam Kadmon, the Tree of Life in the microcosm. This arrangement is surrounded by ten horns, symbols of creative force.

The Beast tramples upon images of the saints, whose purity and chastity denies them the sexual and magickal power shown in this trump. These images, separated by the feet of the Beast, form the letter *Shin*. Shin is the Aeon, the Stèle of Revealing that shows the gods of the New Aeon, as Lust shows Babalon and the Beast, the terrestrial representatives of those gods.

---

30. Crowley, Aleister, *The Book of Lies* (York Beach, ME: Samuel Weiser, 1993), 108–109.
31. Ibid., 109.

Interpretation

In a reading, Lust indicates energy and power in a person or a situation. The lion (Leo) symbolizes the courage and strength necessary to properly harness and direct this energy. Sexual union and sexual power are indicated, but not love—the concept of love falls under the dominion of the Empress. Lust may also signify conception of a child.

When reversed, the energy symbolized in Lust becomes unstable and dissipates, which implies a weakness or inability to control this energy. There may be a lack of enthusiasm and passion for the matter at hand. You may be burned out and require rest to regenerate. Lust reversed may also signify sexual abuse and rape, the perversion of sexual power.

XII. The Hanged Man

Hebrew Letter
Mem

Meaning
Water

Attribution
Water

Path
23rd

Connects
Geburah and Hod

☐ The Hanged Man ▽

The Hanged Man is a glyph of the Adept as the God-Man or Redeemer, inverted and suspended between Kether and Malkuth.

The Adept hangs from an inverted ankh, his left foot secured by a coiled serpent. The ankh is an Egyptian symbol of eternal life, and it projects from the white light of Kether. The ankh also represents the fifth Power of the Sphinx, to Go. The fifth power of the Sphinx can only be realized by an Adept, one who has mastered the other four Powers of the Sphinx: to Know, to Will, to Dare, and to Keep Silent.

Crowley has removed the gallows of traditional design, which was a symbol of suffering and punishment that is inappropriate to his New Aeon reinterpretation of this trump. Eliphas Lévi describes the gallows as having the form of the Hebrew letter Tau,[32] and A. E. Waite shows the Adept hanging from a gallows in the shape of a *T*, which is also Tau. As an acknowledgment of the traditional symbolism, the topmost part of the ankh in the Thoth trump is deep olive-green (the color of Mem in Yetzirah), forming an inverted *T*. Tau is attributed to the Universe card, which signifies the completion of the Great Work.

The serpent that secures the Adept is coiled twice, and its placement below the white light of Kether indicates that it is associated with Chokmah. Chokmah is the creator as the Logos of Kether, yet also the destroyer as the source of duality. The serpent is also associated with Mercury.

---

32. Lévi, Eliphas, *Transcendental Magic* (York Beach, ME: Samuel Weiser, 1999), 391.

The Adept's legs form a cross, and his arms form a triangle. The cross and triangle is the emblem of the Golden Dawn. The triangle is a symbol of light and the cross a symbol of life; together they signify light descending into darkness in order to redeem it. The Adept is therefore the redeemer, who bridges the gap between the spiritual (the light of Kether) and the material (the life manifest in Malkuth). The placement of the head of the Adept in the center of the triangle also suggests the Eye in the Triangle, a symbol of spiritual enlightenment.

The Adept is crucified with nails shaped like the Hebrew letter Vau, which represent the Adept's obligation and role as the redeemer. Like the Hierophant, the redeemer is one who transmits the wisdom and understanding of the Supernals to those below the Abyss. However, this role is not forced upon the Adept—as indicated by the green disks that signify Venus and therefore love—and also by the Vau-nails; for Taurus is attributed to Vau, and of the four Powers of the Sphinx, Taurus represents Will. Together they signify the obligation of the Adept: "Love is the Law, Love under Will" (AL 1:57).

Redemption does not imply the idea of sacrifice commonly associated with this trump. Crowley considered the idea of sacrifice to be an Old Aeon concept, the New Aeon bringing redemption *from* sacrifice. This same interpretation of redemption is also found in the Empress and the Emperor, where the Old Aeon symbols of sacrifice are removed in the process of purification.

Below the Adept is a vesica or womb. Eighteen rays are drawn from the Adept's head to the center of the womb, the numeration of *chai*, Hebrew for "living." The serpent within the vesica is coiled four times, indicating manifestation, and the black waters of the womb allude to Binah, the Great Sea and the Great Fertile Mother. The serpent is roughly black with a yellow crosshatch pattern; black rayed yellow is the color of Malkuth in Assiah, signifying full manifestation. The vesica is the vehicle of manifestation, and the serpent is the illumination of Kether manifesting in Malkuth through the work of the Adept.

Behind the Adept is a grid of small squares. These are the Four Elemental Watchtowers of the Enochian system, which represent the energies that make up the terrestrial universe. The legs of the Adept form a cross over the darker grid of squares, identifying him with the Black Cross of Spirit[33] that separates and binds the Four Elemental Watchtowers.

The horizontal lines in the background are prominent while the vertical lines are faint and blurred, suggesting the reflective and refractive qualities of Water. In this context, the Adept is also the Drowned Man, a title associated with the drowned and resurrected god Osiris, who appears underwater in the next trump, Death.

Interpretation

In a reading, the Hanged Man indicates redemption. There may be an opportunity to redeem yourself in a situation, to repair what was damaged, or to restore what was lost. The watery nature of this trump signifies redemption on a spiritual or emotional level that releases you from blame, guilt, or spiritual transgressions. The descent of spirit into matter, the progression from the white light of Kether to the serpent of Malkuth, often manifests as spiritually motivated altruism and charity.

When reversed, the traditional interpretations of the Hanged Man are present: sacrifice, suffering, and punishment. These characteristics are important elements in the myths of the Old Aeon redeemers Osiris and Christ. You may fall from grace, damaging reputations and relationships. Like the Adept, your world may be literally turned upside down. The reversed trump may also signify a false redeemer, one who manipulates the spiritual for material gain.

---

33.   In the Enochian System of Magick, the Black Cross of Spirit is represented by the Tablet of Union.

The Death card is a glyph of natural change and transformation expressed through the alchemical process of putrefaction.

In the traditional imagery of this trump, the scythe-wielding skeleton is a harvester of men. This iconography is a reflection of the emphasis on death and dying perpetuated in the Aeon of Osiris. In the Aeon of Horus, this concept of death is revealed as an illusion, and thus Crowley's Death trump emphasizes the transformation, the resurrection, and the creation that follow death.

The skeleton represents the agent of putrefaction, the alchemical process in which the first matter is purified through the process of dissolution, decay, and death. Bones are the only part of the human body that remain after the natural forces of decay (putrefaction) have completed their work. The skeleton is black, the color of Saturn, and his legs form the Hebrew letter Tau, which is attributed to Saturn. Saturn, in conjunction with Binah, is associated with the idea of form, and Death is simply the transfer of force from one form to another. Saturn indicates not only structure and form but also the concept of time. Putrefaction is a very long process, especially as it occurs in nature. The skeleton dances to indicate that this is an active process.

The skeleton wears the Crown of Osiris, the Crown of Upper Egypt flanked by the ostrich plumes of Maat.[34] In Egyptian mythology, Osiris is ruler of the dead and the lord of the Egyptian underworld, the waters of the Duat. Osiris is also associated with

---

34.   See the description of the Adjustment trump.

XIII. Death

Hebrew Letter
Nun

Meaning
Fish

Attribution
Scorpio

Path
24th

Connects
Tiphareth and Netzach

the waters of death, for in one Egyptian myth his brother Set drowned him in the Nile. To reflect this connection with Osiris, the skeleton is underwater, as indicated by the swimming fish and the bubbles rising to the surface.

The process of death is symbolized by two human figures framed within the legs of the skeleton. The lower figure is slumped over; it appears thin, frail, and weak. The blade of the scythe crosses the figure's neck, symbolically beheading it. The head represents the Neschamah, the essence of the mind—the higher soul that transcends the self. From the head of the lower figure issues a second figure that rises above the scythe. This figure is more active and alive than the first, and it beholds a bright light before it. The scythe of death releases the immortal soul from the mortal body, allowing it to reincarnate.

Bubbles rise from the skeleton, and these bubbles hold human figures of all ages. In the largest bubbles above the scythe, there is an adult male, an adult female, an infant, and a single sperm. The bubbles are held together by a weave of threads that form the phallus of the skeleton. The phallus is an organ of creation, and its function is to reincarnate these souls in a physical body. With the scythe he destroys life, and with the phallus he creates life.

On the left side of the card are the icons of the tripartite Scorpio: the scorpion, the snake, and the eagle. These icons represent the cycle of death, creation, and incarnation.

The Scorpion stands between a lily and a lotus, plants associated with Binah and Saturn. The lily has the shape of the Greek letter Alpha, and the letter Omega is drawn in light blue on the lotus. These symbols evoke the Saturnine traits of time and limitation, that which has a beginning and an end. The scorpion is trapped between them, signifying the mortality of the physical body.

The Serpent represents the Kundalini serpent that lies coiled at the base of the spine, dormant until aroused by sexual attraction and physical pleasure. The Serpent's tail is in the mouth of a fish. The fish is a feminine symbol by virtue of its shape, and the serpent is phallic. Together they signify the physical union that leads to creation, and thus they are appropriately placed behind the skeleton's phallus of creation.

At the top of the trump is the eagle, which represents the spiritual ecstasy of orgasm that initiates the creation of life. Threads descend from the eagle to connect it to the creative process below, the miracle of incarnation.

The tripartite scorpio also symbolizes the three physical states of matter, the components of the human body that are separated in the process of putrefaction. The scorpion is associated with ice (solid) due to its hard shell. The serpent represents the liquid form of water on account of its flowing movement. The eagle is steam, the gaseous form of water that floats in the air.

Interpretation

In a reading, Death indicates natural change, the natural progression of life through creation, death, and incarnation evident in all living beings. It signifies the passage of time and its effects: children mature, bodies age and decay, rulers and governments come and go, new technologies are developed and make their impact on society. It indicates the logical development of a situation. This trump may suggest that it is time to initiate change in a situation, or to cut away old ideas or habits. The Death card also signifies the need for patience, as natural changes take time.

When reversed, this trump signifies decay and stagnation. You may be trying to force something to happen faster than planned or normally possible, resulting in unnecessary waste or even failure. Like the scorpion, you may feel trapped by time constraints or your limitations. Death reversed may also indicate a fear of death or change, a fear which often traps people in difficult or harmful situations.

XIV. Art

Hebrew Letter
Samekh

Meaning
Tent-prop

Attribution
Sagittarius

Path
25th

Connects
Tiphareth and Yesod

Art is a glyph of synthesis, the alchemical process of *coagula* that follows the process of *solve* illustrated in the Lovers.

This trump was originally titled *Temperance*. The Golden Dawn presented two different versions of this trump in the Portal ritual. One version of Temperance was drawn in the conventional style seen in the Marseilles tarot and popularized by the successful Rider-Waite deck. The traditional design shows an angel pouring water from a golden vase into a silver vase, which symbolizes the integration of Fire and Water, and of the solar and lunar forces. The other version of this trump used more complex alchemical symbolism to depict the synthesis of opposites, and that version of Temperance is the basis for the design of the Thoth trump.

Crowley renamed this trump *Art* because it is an illustration the art of alchemy. The revised title also alludes to Crowley's definition of magick: "The Science and Art of causing change to occur in conformity with Will." The Lovers is a glyph of analysis, the basis of science; its counterpart in this definition of Magick is the alchemical Art.

The Hermetic Marriage that took place in the Lovers is now complete, and the Black King and the White Queen have merged to become a single androgynous figure. The head of the Black King has the blond hair and silver crown of the White Queen. Likewise, the head of the White Queen has the dark hair and golden crown of the Black King. The transpositions that occur everywhere in this trump signify the complete integration of opposites.

The Androgyne wears a blue lamen over her solar plexus; the lamen is the magickal weapon of

Tiphareth. This lamen is inscribed with six visible spheres, symbolic of the six planetary Sephiroth that are below the Abyss on the Tree of Life. The spheres on the lamen are also breasts, identifying the Androgyne with Diana, the many-breasted Roman goddess of fertility and the Moon. Thus the lamen is both solar and lunar in nature, symbolizing yet another union of opposites.

The arrow of Sagittarius is placed in the sphere corresponding to Yesod, and it points to Tiphareth, indicating the position of the path of Samekh on the Tree of Life. In the Golden Dawn system of initiation, the path of Samekh leads from the outer order elemental grades to the Adeptus Minor grade in Tiphareth. In this context, the Androgyne represents the Adept, showing her Higher Self realized and integrated with her physical self.

The Androgyne's robe is green, indicating the fertility implicit in the union of the King and Queen. It is adorned with the same serpents and bees found on the robes of the King and Queen in the Lovers, and the bees and serpents together represent the fertility that renews the cycle of life.

The Androgyne pours Water and Fire into the cauldron, her forearms counterchanged with the colors of the heads. The colors of the lion and the eagle have also been transposed, and they stand upon burning water, symbolic of the union and integration of Fire and Water. The white lion pours his red blood into the cauldron, and the red eagle adds her white gluten. In alchemical terms, the Red Tincture of the Emperor and the White Tincture of the Empress have been combined with alchemical Mercury (symbolized by the rainbow) to form the Philosopher's Stone.

The cauldron represents the newly made Adept or Androgyne. The elements of the Adept, having been analyzed, balanced, and purified in previous cards, are here re-integrated into the whole. The cauldron is the yellow-gold of Tiphareth and the Sun, which reflects the balance and harmony of the elements therein. The cross and skull are symbols associated with Saturn and Tau, the letter of the path below Samekh on the Tree of Life. The Tau cross on the rim of the cauldron symbolizes the harmonious union of the five elements. The raven perched upon a skull signifies the *caput mortuum*, Latin for "dead head," the dross of this alchemical operation. This also indicates the death of orgasm that results in the mixture of the sexual fluids, the blood and the gluten within the cauldron.

Energy and light rise from the cauldron, following the arrow of Sagittarius that signifies the aspiration of the True Will of the Androgyne. The arrow of Samekh is propelled upward by the bow of *Qesheth*, the Hebrew word for "bow," formed from the letters of the three paths rising from Malkuth: Qoph, Shin, and Tau. The stream of energy rising from the cauldron transforms into a rainbow that forms the cape of the Androgyne. The word *Qesheth* also means rainbow, and the rainbow is a symbol or enlightenment, the light of the Sun (consciousness) shining through the waters of the unconscious—yet another union of opposites.

The lunar crescents at the top of the card allude to the Moon and Gimel, the path above Samekh on the Middle Pillar. The crescents crown the Androgyne—Gimel being the path that leads to Kether, the crown. These crescents also form the bow of Artemis, the goddess of the Moon and hunters.

At the top of the trump is written "Visita Interiora Terrae Rectificando Invenies Occultum Lapidem," Latin for "Visit the interior parts of the Earth; by rectification thou shalt find the Hidden Stone." The initial letters of this sentence form the word vitriol, which is the universal solvent formed by the perfect balance of the alchemical elements of Sulfur, Salt, and Mercury.[35] The "Hidden Stone" is the Philosopher's Stone of the alchemists, representative of the true self and the accomplishment of the Great Work. The Stone can only be found within the aspirant, the "interior parts of the Earth" that are purified by the application of vitriol, the universal solvent.

The keyword of this sentence is "rectification," the alchemical process of purification through repeated distillation. The word Rectificando is separated from the rest of the formula by the lunar crescents to emphasize the importance of this process. From this perspective, the trump symbolically illustrates the process of distillation. The First Matter is placed in a flask (cauldron) with an extracting fluid such as alcohol, which has the qualities of both fire and water. It is heated with an even flame to emulate the power of the Sun. The subtle essence of the First Matter rises and condenses in another vessel, precipitating like a rainbow, while the dross remains in the flask below.

Interpretation

In a reading, Art indicates union and synthesis. It may signify teamwork and cooperation, combining resources to accomplish a particular purpose or goal. On a more personal level, the Androgyne symbolizes the rectification and integration of the dif-

---

35. Crowley, *The Book of Thoth*, 104.

ferent parts of the self, the union of the conscious mind and the unconscious mind; the emotions and the intellect; and the mind, body, and spirit. This trump also indicates moderation, a healthy balance between two opposites or extremes.

When reversed, Art signifies the clash of opposites; the fire boils away the water and the water extinguishes the fire. Differences and dissension may disrupt or fragment a group. Competition between rivals is also indicated. Trauma may disrupt the harmony between the different parts of the self. The reversed trump may also signify a lack of moderation or self-restraint that leads to a harmful imbalance, excess, or deficiency.

XV. The Devil

Hebrew Letter

Ayin

Meaning

Eye

Attribution

Capricorn

Path

26th

Connects

Tiphareth and Hod

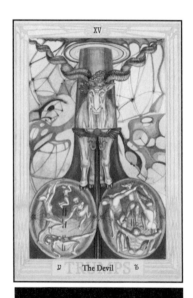

The Devil is a glyph of primal urges and instincts, the basic impulses to survive and reproduce symbolized by the goat and the phallus.

Traditionally, the goat-headed figure portrayed in the Devil is connected with the Christian devil. Crowley offers a more positive interpretation of the goat:

> *Now the Path of Ayin is a link between Mercury and the Sun, and in the Zodiac importeth the Goat. This Goat is called also Strength, and standeth in the Meridian at the Sunrise of Spring, and it is his Nature to leap upon the Mountains . . . Now the Goat flieth not as doth the Eagle; but consider this also, that it is the true Nature of Man to dwell upon the Earth, so that his Flights are oft but Phantasy; yea, the Eagle also is bound to his Eyrie, nor feedeth upon Air. Therefore this Goat, making each Leap with Fervour, yet at all Times secure in his own Element, is a true Hieroglyph of the Magician.*[36]

At the center of the card is a goat with spiral horns and a third eye in his forehead. The goat represents Pan Pangenetor, the All-Begetter, and Baphomet, the symbolic icon of the life-force. The horns symbolize masculine energy and virility. Their spiral shape alludes to the universal pattern or structure of energy that is evident in all levels of nature, from

---

36. Crowley, Aleister, *Liber Aleph vel CXI: The Book of Wisdom or Folly* (York Beach, ME: Samuel Weiser, 1991), chapter 174.

the helix of DNA to spiral galaxies. When the primal procreative energy of the Devil is tapped into and directed, it results in the powerful magick depicted in Lust.

The third eye of the goat is symbolic of spiritual enlightenment, the opening of the Ajna chakra. The eye is also the phallus, as it resembles the head of the phallus. Above the eye and between the horns are grapes, suggestive of the orgiastic mysteries of Dionysus or Bacchus. These grapes are also found in the Fool, which depicts the creative potential of the universe.

In front of the goat is the Wand of the Chief Adept, a specific form of the caduceus. The Wand of the Chief Adept appears in the Adeptus Minor Ritual of the Golden Dawn, where it is used to invoke the element of Spirit. Two serpents flank the winged solar orb, symbolizing sperm. The serpents wear the crowns of Upper and Lower Egypt, alluding to the unification of the Two Lands of Egypt as a metaphor for the harmonious unification of opposites.

The caduceus is a symbol of creative energy; it also represents the winged (erect) phallus. The caduceus also appears in the Fool, the first creative impulse, and the Magus, the Will. In this context, it is analogous with the Chiah, the creative impulse and divine will.

The tree trunk and the spheres below it obviously represent the erect phallus and testicles, the organs of male creative force. The trunk penetrates the rings of Saturn, the ruler of Capricorn. The rings also represent Nuit, who is associated with Saturn as Binah, the Great Mother.[37]

The male and female forms within the spheres represent the possible forms aspiring to be created by the sexual act. There are four female figures in the left sphere. Three women adore the goat while a fourth lies prostrate. In the right sphere are three male figures, in poses of adoration and aspiration, who are being subdued by a Minotaur. The Minotaur is found in the Greek legend of Pasiphae, and here it represents the potential god-man or messiah created by the sexual union of the mortal woman Pasiphae and the divine bull of Poseidon.

These spheres are also cells, the building blocks of living matter, dividing to create life. Each contains ten pairs of chromosomes, or twenty marks; both numbers are associated with Yod, the spermatozoa that are generated in the testicles.

---

37. See the description of the Star trump.

Behind the tree is a chaotic root-design on a pale red background. Lady Harris associates these markings with the Martian canals, indicating that the background is the surface of the planet Mars, which is exalted in Capricorn.[38] Mars governs sexual energies and the sex drive found in all beings.

Interpretation

In a reading, the Devil signifies the instinctual creative impulse. It symbolizes the sexual attraction and arousal that compels us to form relationships and procreate. The influence of Capricorn indicates drive, determination, and ambition. This card also represents competition, the desire to win, and the motivation to improve.

When the Devil is reversed, the instincts take over, and the temptation becomes too powerful to resist. Thus it indicates infidelity, lust of the flesh, and the negative consequences of violating sexual taboos in society. Impulsive and compulsive behavior may lead you to act without thinking, actions that will be regretted later. The Devil symbolizes the "flight or fight" instinct, and therefore may indicate the violent behavior associated with the Minotaur. The competitive, violent, and impulsive nature of this card may also indicate criminal activity.

---

38. Wasserman, James. *Instructions for Aleister Crowley's Thoth Tarot Deck,* 42.

The Tower is a glyph of purification through destruction, expressed through the fiery, destructive energy of Mars.

At the top of the trump is the Eye of Horus, shown destroying the Old Aeon (symbolized by the Tower) by fire. In affirming this connection with the solar god Horus, the sigil of the Sun is drawn in black as the pupil of the Eye. Twenty-seven rays radiate from the Solar Eye, and the Tower is attributed to the 27th path on the Tree of Life.

The Eye is also associated with the third eye of the goat in the Devil. The opening of the third eye chakra results in the destruction of illusion through enlightenment. The tower symbolizes the conscious mind or the ego, which is destroyed by the lightning flash of spiritual illumination.

Behind the Eye is the lightning bolt, a symbol of destruction and of enlightenment. The lightning bolt that strikes the base of the tower has five points, the number of Geburah and Mars.

The tower represents the physical world of Malkuth, signified by the two barred windows of the tower. The lower window is divided into ten squares, the number of Malkuth. The upper window, a circle divided by a diagonal cross, suggests the saltire of the four elements in Malkuth.

Four figures fall from the tower, painted black to identify them with the element of Earth. The garrison is drawn in an abstract form to mimic the crystalline structures of rocks and minerals. This alludes to their traditional relationship with Ayin and Capricorn, the sign of cardinal Earth in the zodiac.

XVI. The Tower

Hebrew Letter
Pé

Meaning
Mouth

Attribution
Mars

Path
27th

Connects
Netzach and Hod

In the sexual interpretation of these symbols, the tower represents the phallus, the lightning flash represents the orgasm, and the garrison represents the ejaculated sperm. The tower is destroyed, signifying the loss of erection that comes after orgasm. It is noteworthy that the letter Pé was used in Crowley's diaries to signify oral sex, *Pé* meaning "mouth" and the Tower representing the phallus.[39]

At the bottom of the card is Dis, the Roman god of the underworld commonly associated with the Greek god Hades. Dis is represented as a mouth (the meaning of Pé) breathing forth destructive fire at the foundation of the tower. *Tooth* in Hebrew is "shin," the element of Fire represented by the flames shooting from his mouth.

Nine tongues of flame belch forth from his mouth, the number of Yesod. Crowley refers to Pé as the roof of Yesod,[40] and the value of the letter Pé is eighty, the same value as the word *Yesod*. Yesod is the Foundation of the Tree, yet the Moon and Air are both attributed to the Sephira. This relationship alludes to the idea that change is stability and inertia is death. That which will not change is destroyed and dies.

The dove and serpent are linked to the Tower in *The Book of the Law*:

> *Love is the law, love under will. Nor let the fools mistake love; for there are love and love. There is the dove, and there is the serpent. Choose ye well! He, my prophet, hath chosen, knowing the law of the fortress, and the great mystery of the House of God* (AL I:57).

The dove represents the Holy Ghost of Christian theology, fleeing the destruction of the Old Aeon. The dove bearing an olive branch is a symbol of peace, which is driven off by war (*War* is the alternate title of this trump.)

The dove is succeeded by the lion-serpent moving toward the center of the card. The lion-serpent is of the same design as that found in Lust, where it symbolizes the phallus engaged a powerful act of sexual magick. The dove is a symbol of Old Aeon Christianity, and the lion-serpent symbolizes the New Aeon of Horus.

Crowley identifies the serpent as Abraxas. The divine name Abraxas enumerates to 365, the number of days in the solar year and a great secret in ancient times.

The serpent is surrounded by a nimbus of fifteen rays, the numeration of Hod spelled in full. Likewise, the Dove is a symbol of Venus and Netzach. The path of Pé

---

39. Crowley, Aleister, *The Magical Record of the Beast 666* (ed. John Symonds and Kenneth Grant, London: Gerald Duckworth & Co., 1993), 45.
40. Crowley, *The Vision and the Voice*, 73, footnote 1.

bridges Hod and Netzach; it is where the intellect and the emotions clash. The enlightenment and illumination that resolves this conflict is symbolized by the Solar Eye, the Sun of Tiphareth.

Interpretation

In a reading, the Tower indicates a sudden and unexpected change, often a traumatic event that leads to a better situation in the long run. For example, you may lose your job only to find better employment, or break up with a lover and later realize that the relationship was stifling your personal growth. The Tower also brings purification through destruction, which is stressful but also beneficial—such as when one is forced to abandon beliefs or opinions in light of new experiences. The import of the tower can be likened to an old building that is torn down so that a new structure may take its place.

When reversed, the Tower symbolizes danger, injury, and disaster, often physical in nature. It also indicates resistance to inevitable and obvious change, such as the resistance of orthodoxy to the evolution of society and culture. The clash between emotions and intellect may bring confusion and pain, especially when reacting to sudden change. Fighting, conflict, and war are also characteristics of this trump, qualities of the attribution of Mars.

XVII. The Star

Hebrew Letter
Hé

Meaning
Window

Attribution
Aquarius

Path
28th

Connects
Chokmah and Tiphareth

The Star is a glyph of reincarnation and the renewal of life.

In *The Book of Thoth*, Crowley refers to the central figure as Nuith, a variant of the more common spelling of Nuit.[41] Nuith adds up to 466, the same value as *Olam ha-Yetzirah*, "The World of Formation." When the four Qabalistic Worlds are mapped onto a single Tree of Life, Yetzirah is attributed to Sephiroth four through nine, where the energies of the Qabala become manifest. Thus Nuith is Nuit shown in manifestation.

The placement of Nuit in this card also suggests manifestation. The figure in the traditional design of the Star stands with one foot on land and one foot on water. The water behind Nuit is the Great Sea of Binah, and before her is the manifest universe, symbolized by the crystalline earth. If Nuit stands with one foot on land and one on water, she bridges the Abyss, bringing the unmanifested powers of the Supernals into manifestation. Likewise, the path of Hé connects Chokmah to Tiphareth and spans the Abyss.

This depiction of Nuit resembles the image of Aquarius the water-bearer, the zodiacal sign attributed to this trump. This figure also bears characteristics of the Egyptian goddess Nut, who is commonly represented by a woman with a vase of water on her head. As a hieroglyph, this image signifies the word *Nu*, a name often substituted for Nuit in *The Book of the Law*.[42]

---

41.   Crowley, *The Book of Thoth*, 109.
42.   For example: AL 2:1, 2, 43, 64.

The gold and silver cups symbolize the solar and lunar forces. The light of the Sun is absorbed and reflected by the Moon to the Earth. Similarly, the force of Chokmah impregnates the Great Womb of Binah, which gives birth to manifestation below the Abyss; the Yod initiates the current of energy, and the Primal Hé absorbs, reflects, and transmits it.

From the golden cup, Nuit pours the Water of Universal Life, the essence of all life, upon herself. In humanity, this essence is the soul, which does not die but reincarnates. This life-energy fills the womb of Nuit to manifest as life on Earth. Energy spirals out of the golden cup, appearing as water and as light. At the center of the spiral is a small blue seven-pointed star, the star of Venus, symbolizing the love that is inherent within the Water of Universal Life.

From the silver cup, Nuit pours the Water of Universal Life upon the fertile earth. Here the life-energy takes form in the manifest universe. The crystalline earth in the foreground is made up of seven twenty-sided translucent solids. They are seven in number to indicate the influence of Venus; the twenty sides are a reference to Yod, the Hermit, representing the fertile earth unrealized and unfulfilled. It is the Water of Universal Life pouring out of the silver cup that bestows life unto the material world.

Flying upward from the lower right of the card are five butterflies. The butterfly is a symbol of Psyche, the soul. In this trump, the butterflies symbolize souls that have traversed the Abyss to be reborn in the womb of Babalon. They have been stripped of the ego, the Ruach; the quintessential quality of the Adept, the soul or Neschamah, is all that remains. The butterflies are five in number to identify them with the fifth element of Spirit.

Beneath the butterflies are three red roses, symbolic of the fertile earth. The rose is also associated with Venus as a symbol of love. On the distant shore is the City of the Pyramids in Binah, the dwelling-place of the Adepts who have crossed the Abyss.

The globe behind Nuit is actually her reflection across the Abyss, the Primium Mobile of Chokmah. Within the globe is the Star of Venus. The influence of the Star of Venus spirals out to encompass the entire globe. Venus appears above the Abyss in the Empress trump.

Outside the Primium Mobile, or known universe, is the Star of Babalon, a seven-pointed star with seven numeral 7s inscribed therein. The Star of Babalon reconciles and unites all of the major symbolism of this card. Babalon is identified with Nuit in *The Book of the Law*: "Now, therefore, I am known to ye by my name Nuit, and to him by a secret name which I will give him when at last he knoweth me" (AL 1:22). Crowley informs us in his commentary to chapter 49 of *The Book of Lies* that this secret name is Babalon.[43]

Babalon resides in Binah, above the Abyss, where she is the Lady of the City of the Pyramids and is identified as the Great Mother. She is associated with Venus, and her name is written with seven 7s in a seven-pointed star, seven being the number of Netzach and Venus. The influence of the Star of Babalon reaches throughout the entire card, its rays of spiritual light spiraling out behind even the globe.

Interpretation

In a reading, the Star indicates hope and faith, beliefs fostered by the spiritual concepts of reincarnation, renewal, and the beneficent nature of the universe. Baptism and purification are also associated with these spiritual concepts. This is the trump of meditation and reflection, methods of exploring and examining your inner self.

The Star reversed signifies disbelief and skepticism. It indicates an unwillingness to examine yourself and your behavior, often due to a fear of what you may find or may have to confront when you look inside. The reversed trump may also symbolize deception and may refer to one who is gullible or naïve, and thus easily taken advantage of.

---

43. Crowley, *The Book of Lies*, 109.

The Moon is a glyph of illusion and deception associated with the unconscious mind and the astral plane. While the Priestess represents the most exalted characteristics of the Moon, the Moon trump represents the darker, more sinister aspects of the Moon.

At the bottom of the card is a beetle bearing the solar disk, an icon of the Egyptian god Khephra, who represents the Sun at midnight. The Sun is a symbol of the conscious mind, which has descended into the dark waters of the unconscious to confront the neuroses, fears, and other unresolved emotions that lie within. The water is tinged with blue and red tidal graphs to indicate the influence of the Moon on the waters of the unconscious mind.

Guarding the pathway or stream that runs between the turrets and the mountains is Anubis in his dual form, which is defined in the Neophyte Ceremony of the Golden Dawn as "Anubis of the East" and "Anubis of the West," the guardians of the Neophyte Hall.[44] They guard the threshold between the conscious and the unconscious mind, turning back those who are not ready to confront the horrors and demons of the unconscious. The neophyte who ignores the dire warning of Anubis risks being devoured by the Nephesch, the animal soul symbolized by the two jackals. The Nephesch is the Qabalistic Part of the Soul that is seated in Yesod, the Moon, and is associated with the cerebellum at the back of the head, the meaning of Qoph.

XVIII. The Moon

Hebrew Letter
Qoph

Meaning
Back of head

Attribution
Pisces

Path
29th

Connects
Netzach and Malkuth

---

44. Regardie, *The Golden Dawn*, 341.

A visual examination of the figure in the left side of the trump reveals his features to be more like that of Set than Anubis, having a narrower snout, longer ears, and a longer neck characteristic of the mysterious Set-animal. Set was the Egyptian god of the desert, storms, and darkness, a strong and virile god demonized by the Osirian cult as the murderer of Osiris. Set represents the strength, energy, and courage required to defeat the demons of the unconscious mind. Anubis acts as guide through the darkness, the psychopomp of the path of Qoph.

The ankh that Set holds is actually the sigil of the planet Mercury, the planet that is in its detriment in Pisces. The rational and logical intellect is of little use in the realm of the unconscious. Anubis holds a composite symbol formed from the sigils of Neptune (the ruler of Pisces) and Venus (exalted in Pisces), more concurrent with the energies of the Moon trump. Set and Anubis each hold a Phoenix Wand, a symbol of resurrection.

Nine Yod-shaped drops of blood fall from the Moon at the top of the trump, the number of Yesod, the Sephira of the Astral Plane and the Moon. This blood is menstrual blood, one of the perfumes attributed to the path of Qoph.[45] The Yod represents the latent potential seed of life; as menstrual blood, it symbolizes the fact that its potential has been unfulfilled and the unfertilized egg has been ejected. This occurs in the symbolic womb formed by the mountains and turrets. Note also that Virgo (Yod) is opposite Pisces on the wheel of the zodiac.

The Yods of blood form the sigil of Neptune, the ruler of Pisces. The darker aspects of Neptune correspond with concepts associated with the Moon trump: dreams, illusion, delusion, fog, mystery, confusion, trances, addictions, hypnosis, and sleepwalking.

At the top of the card is the crescent Moon. It is symbolically the waning Moon, but it would only appear in the sky as portrayed in the card during a partial eclipse of the Moon. Thus, the bluish sphere is the Earth, separating the Sun and the Moon.

The Hebrew letter Kaph is inscribed in crimson within the Earth-sphere. It shows the influence of Jupiter, which, with Neptune, is the ruler of Pisces. Crimson is the color of Pisces in Atziluth, and the path of Qoph leads upwards to the path of Kaph. These attributions indicate that the aspirant may invoke the aspiration and faith of Jupiter for strength on the journey through the darkness of the unconscious mind.

---

45.   Crowley, *777 and Other Qabalistic Writings*, 121.

Interpretation

In a reading, the Moon indicates illusion and delusion. Unconscious desires and repressed feelings may interfere with the situation at hand. The demons of the unconscious may manifest in our lives as neurosis, depression, and insanity. The infertile womb depicted in this trump signifies rejection, unrealized plans, and personal crisis.

When reversed, the Moon signifies acknowledging and dealing with the demons of the unconscious mind. Like Khephra, who as a solar god is symbolic of the conscious mind, we descend into the darkness of the unconscious to fight the monsters within. This may be accomplished alone or with the help of friends, family, or therapy.

XIX. The Sun

Hebrew Letter
Resh

Meaning
Head

Attribution
The Sun

Path
30th

Connects
Hod and Yesod

The Sun is a glyph of emancipation and freedom, principles associated with the dawning of the Aeon of Horus.

The Sun at the center of this trump represents Heru-Ra-Ha, the composite name of Horus from *The Book of the Law*. Within the solar disk is a rose, corresponding to the symbol of the Rose Cross. In the Sun trump, Crowley redefines the symbol of the Rose Cross in the context of the New Aeon, replacing the conventional four-armed cross with a star of twelve rays.[46] The four-armed cross symbolizes the union of the terrestrial elements, four being the number of manifestation and limitation. The twelve-rayed star corresponds with the twelve signs of the zodiac, which are representative of the limitless universe and the body of Nuit. Thus, Crowley expands the scope of the symbol of the Rose Cross from the limitation of the terrestrial universe to the infinite freedom of the celestial universe.

The rays of the Sun separate the signs of the zodiac at the rim of the card; its shorter rays divide each sign into decans. The figures of the zodiac are drawn in the corresponding colors of Atziluth; thus they bear forth their highest and most spiritual qualities. The signs of the zodiac are placed in a rainbow, which symbolizes the energy of the Sun manifest through Water, symbolic of enlightened consciousness. The Sun rises over a green mound, which is symbolic of the fertile earth.

Two children dance joyfully in front of the mound. The male child is red, representing Fire, while the female child is yellow, the color of Air.

---

46. Crowley, *The Book of Thoth*, 114.

The children have butterfly wings. In the Star, the butterfly is a symbol of the soul; here, the souls of the male and female are shown liberated and free. The children are shown with arms thrown up and legs crossed. This is a reversal of the pose of the Hanged Man, and it signifies their release from the sacrifice and suspension traditionally symbolized by that trump. From a Thelemic perspective, the children are Heru-Ra-Ha manifest in his dual form: Ra-Hoor-Khuit as the red child (Fire), and Harpocrates as the yellow child (Air).

The children dance upon two disks, the darkest symbols in the trump. Each disk is inscribed with a figure crucified upon a Tau cross. The disks represent the Christian formula of the Rose and Cross, Christ being a sacred sign of the Old Aeon. It also alludes to the attribution of the dying or sacrificed god attributed to Tiphareth, the Sun.

The disks are blue and green, representing the passive elements found in the Golden Dawn version of the trump, where they signify the generating influence of Water and Earth.[47] From the blue disk (Water) rises the red child (Fire). Likewise from the green disk (Earth) comes the yellow child (Air). This relationship between the elements symbolizes the triumph of the Aeon of Horus over the Aeon of Osiris. The red and yellow wall that surrounds the mound also signifies the active elements of Air and Fire, working together in harmony.

Interpretation

In a reading, the Sun indicates freedom and emancipation. You may be released from an obligation or debt, allowed to make your own decisions, or empowered to pursue your own destiny. The children represent happiness and good health, and their pose symbolizes the freedom to act or choose. The attribution of the Sun also signifies riches, glory, and success.

When reversed, the children in the Sun resume the pose of the traditional Hanged Man, and thus the card indicates the loss of freedom and choice. You may be taking advantage of your rights without acknowledging the rules and responsibilities that come with them. Material and emotional stress, symbolized by the blue and green disks, may be interfering with your happiness and health. The reversed trump also indicates health problems, poverty, and shame.

---

47. Regardie, *The Golden Dawn*, 175.

XX. The Aeon

Hebrew Letter
Shin

Meaning
Tooth

Attributions
Fire and Spirit

Path
31st

Connects
Hod and Malkuth

The Aeon is a glyph of change on the highest and deepest levels, often spiritual or universal in nature. Crowley compares the magnitude of this change to the Equinox of the Gods, when the Aeon of Horus succeeded the Aeon of Osiris. Thus he replaces the traditional design of Judgement with that of the Stèle of Revealing, the Egyptian funerary stele that became the herald of the Aeon of Horus and a symbol of Thelemic power.

This trump shows a different perspective of the Stèle. In the Stèle of Revealing, the perspective is that of an observer—we watch as Egyptian scribe Ankh-af-na-Khonsu approaches Ra-Hoor-Khuit, with Nuit and Hadit present. In the Aeon, we take the place of Ankh-af-na-Khonsu; the perspective is that of direct experience, for we are living in the Aeon of Horus.

Framing the card is the arched body of Nuit, who is portrayed in a more abstract form than that which is shown in the Stèle. Her nipples are spiral galaxies, and below her breasts is a girdle decorated with spheres, representing the planets. She wears anklets decorated with a spiked pattern and bracelets decorated with a wavy pattern, signifying the known and the infinite.

Between her hands and feet is Hadit, who is symbolized by the winged globe. The winged globe is the head of the Caduceus Wand, and Shin is the Mother letter that crowns that wand. The winged globe also represents the erect phallus, as indicated in the Magus and the Devil. The serpents coiled beneath the phallic disk are testicles, and the serpents themselves symbolize sperm. In this context, this trump shows the phallus of Hadit penetrating the womb of Nuit.

Unlike his counterparts, Ra-Hoor-Khuit is shown almost exactly as he appears on the Stèle. One element of the Stèle has been corrected in accordance to *The Book of the Law*: "... but my left hand is empty, for I have crushed an universe, & nought remains" (AL III:72). On the Stèle of Revealing, Ra-Hoor-Khuit is depicted holding the Wand of Double Power in his left hand; his right hand is clenched. But in the Aeon he holds the wand in his right hand, while his left hand is empty and open.

Drawn to imply invisibility, Harpocrates stands at the forefront of the trump, as if he were a projection of the visible Ra-Hoor-Khuit. His nakedness signifies his innocence and youth. He gives the Sign of Silence, the gesture with which he is associated.

Harpocrates wears an elaborate headdress crowned with horns that twist out horizontally like those of the ram-headed Khnum, an Egyptian creator-god. Two serpents flank the horns, symbolic of the positive and negative currents of energy harnessed within the child. The base of the headdress is a nemyss, which is secured by a third serpent coiled around the head of Harpocrates. This serpent's head rests just above the god's Ajna chakra, or third eye, signifying power and enlightenment. The side-lock of hair that falls down to his right shoulder is an Egyptian symbol of youth.

Harpocrates stands on the letter Shin, gold in color in accordance with the solar symbolism. Within the Yods of the letter, three figures kneel in prayer. This reminds us that this path does double duty, attributed to the elements of Fire and Spirit. The figure on the right is the father; on the left, the mother; in the center, brighter than his parents, is the child. The Aeon of Horus is the Aeon of the Crowned and Conquering Child, the son of the rulers of the previous Aeons of Isis and Osiris.

The background behind Nuit is the glowing orange-red of Shin in Atziluth. The background behind the letter Shin in this image is the symbolic representation of Libra, the scales. Libra is attributed to Adjustment, which portrays Maat, the ruler of the next Aeon. The placement of the symbol of Libra at the bottom of the card is significant, for Egyptian gods were often depicted standing on or enthroned upon a hieroglyph of Maat, symbolizing their foundation in truth, justice, and order.

The blue and pale green bands are colors of Libra in Briah and Assiah. The orange-red and scarlet band (flecked by the golden shin) is the colors Fire in Atziluth and Yetzirah. A jagged line runs through the orange-red band, signifying the activity of Fire, the initiator of change.

Interpretation

In a reading, the Aeon indicates a personal decision that has a significant impact on your life. For example, you may decide to quit smoking and take better care of your body, or you may pursue a new career. This trump may also signify a life-changing experience, such as a profound spiritual experience or a close brush with death that changes your perspective on life.

If the Aeon is reversed, the decision will have a negative impact on your life. You may fall into a self-destructive lifestyle of addiction, or you could be unsuccessful in your new career. You may suffer a personal defeat, fail to meet personal goals, or be forced to make a decision that violates your ethics or beliefs. The Aeon reversed can also signify psychological issues or trauma that could interfere with your ability to make important life decisions.

The Universe is a glyph of final manifestation and the completion of the Great Work.

A maiden dances in the center of the card. She is shown in the same pose as the children in the Sun trump: legs crossed, arms thrown upwards. As with the reversal of the pose of the Hanged Man, it signifies her freedom to choose and to act.

The maiden's legs form a cross, which is the meaning of the letter Tau. The Tau cross signifies the balance of the four elements and the four letters of the Tetragrammaton. Her legs are crossed in the center of the trump, corresponding with the Kerubim at the corners of the card, symbols also connected with the four elements. This indicates the alignment of the microcosm (elements) and macrocosm (zodiac).

The maiden radiates a square-shaped nimbus of light. The nimbus is symbolic of spiritual exaltation and enlightenment, and the square is a symbol of matter and manifestation. Together they signify the exaltation of spirit in matter.

The symbolism of the maiden and the serpent as a whole is explained in Eliphas Lévi's *Transcendental Magic*:

> *Two things, as we have shewn, are necessary for the acquisition of magical power—the emancipation of will from servitude and its instruction in the art of domination. The sovereign will is represented in our symbols by the Woman who crushes the serpent's head and by the radiant angel who restrains and constrains the dragon with lance and heel. In this place let us affirm that the Great*

XXI. The Universe

Hebrew Letter
Tau

Meaning
Cross

Attributions
Saturn and Earth

Path
32nd

Connects
Yesod and Malkuth

Magical Agent—the double current of light, the living and astral fire of the earth—was represented by the serpent with the head of an ox, goat, or dog, in ancient theogenies. It is the dual serpent of the caduceus, the old serpent of Genesis, but it is also the brazen serpent of Moses, twined about the Tau, that is, the generating lingam ... [It] is really that blind force which souls must overcome if they would be freed from the chains of earth; for, unless their will can detach them from this fatal attraction, they will be absorbed in the current by the force which produced them, and will return to the central and eternal fire. The whole magical work consists therefore in our liberation from the folds of the ancient serpent, then in setting foot upon its head and leading it where we will.[48]

Lévi stresses that the Great Magical Agent or life-energy is a neutral, blind force that may be used for good or for evil.[49] The serpent in this trump reflects this duality in the properties of its two coils: within the first coil is solar light, and within the second coil is darkness. The same duality is also found in the Caduceus Wand, which symbolizes the positive and negative currents of energy (the serpents) dominated and directed by the will (the winged orb).

Lévi also identifies this serpent with the serpent of Genesis, which leads to a different interpretation of the symbolism of this trump. In the Bible, Eve's temptation by the serpent led to the expulsion of Adam and Eve from the Garden of Eden, otherwise known as the Fall of Man. In the Universe trump, we see Eve (the Maiden) as the redeemer of humankind, crushing the head of the serpent that deceived her.

In Genesis, the serpent was condemned to crawl upon the earth; in the Universe, the serpent is black, rayed yellow—the color of Malkuth in Assiah, the lowest Sephira in the Four Qabalistic Worlds. Therefore this serpent is a symbol of both attributions of this trump: it represents the life-energy of Binah, which is Saturn; and its coloration links it with Malkuth and Earth.

The serpent crosses the Maiden at her second chakra, which rules and regulates the sexual functions; in this sense, it represents the Kundalini serpent. In a sexual context, the serpent represents sperm, ejaculated from the eye (Ayin), which is symbolic of the phallus as described in the Devil. The eye is similar in appearance to the

---

48.   Lévi, *Transcendental Magic*, 242–243.
49.   Ibid., 75.

eye found in the Tower, also associated with the ejaculating phallus. It is through the impregnation of the Daughter (the Final Hé of Malkuth and Earth) that she becomes the Mother (the Primal Hé of Binah and Saturn) and the cycle of the Tetragrammaton is renewed.

Crowley identifies the serpent as Heru-Ra-Ha from the Sun trump.[50] The eye is the Eye of Horus, and in this sense the serpent Heru-Ra-Ha is an extension of the eye. The eye is placed adjacent to the Kerub of Aquarius, and the Age of Aquarius roughly corresponds with the Aeon of Horus. Nine rays of blue, red, and yellow emanate from the Eye, colors corresponding to the three primary elements of Water, Fire, and Air. A total of eleven rays radiate from the Eye, the number of Nuit and magick.

The Maiden and serpent dance within a circular grid of stars, the body of Nuit. This grid is seventy-two units in circumference and three units deep, for a total of 216 units. The number 216 is the number of letters in Exodus 14:19–21, the verses that are manipulated to form the names of the Angels of the Shemhamphorash, which rule the thirty-six decans of the zodiac and the thirty-six suit cards of the tarot. The Shemhamphorash is the complete name of God, the full extension of the Tetragrammaton symbolized by the crossed legs of the maiden.

Like the figures of the zodiac in the Sun, the grid is tinted with the colors of the zodiacal signs in Atziluth. There is no apparent pattern to the stars in the grid, and they do not correspond with the star-patterns of the zodiac.

The green sphere behind the Maiden is the planet Earth, which is attributed to this trump. The strange whorl in the center of the sphere is an abstract form of the scarf of traditional design, and thus it is bright blue tinged with yellow, the color of Kaph in Assiah.

Below the Maiden and serpent is the table of the chemical elements, the building blocks of all manifestation. Behind the table of the chemical elements are three pyramids, suggestive of the Pyramids of Giza and therefore the Mysteries of Egypt. Like the table of the chemical elements, the pyramid is a symbol of manifestation and matter.

At the corners of the trump are the four Kerubim. The Kerubim are arranged in the same pattern found in the Hierophant, but here they are winged, and they face outward with wind issuing from their mouths and nostrils. The winds are expres-

---

50.   Crowley, *The Book of Thoth*, 118.

sions of Air, an attribution of the Fool. The Kerubim represent the four elements of the established universe, the same idea that is expressed in the Tau cross. They also represent the four Powers of the Sphinx fully realized and mastered.

The order of the Kerubim does not correspond to the belt of the zodiac; Scorpio and Aquarius are transposed. However, each Kerub does bear a numerological key linking it with the trump sharing its zodiacal attribution. There are thirteen short feathers surrounding the head of the eagle; trump XIII is Death, attributed to Scorpio. The Man bears the numerals 1 and 7 on his ears; trump XVIII is the Star, attributed to Aquarius. The Lion has eleven locks of hair; trump XI, Lust, is attributed to Leo. Finally, the Bull has five locks of hair; trump V is the Hierophant, attributed to Taurus.

This arrangement of the kerubic trumps suggests the life cycle associated with Saturn: Lust is a glyph of conception and birth; the Hierophant shows the mysteries of life; Death indicates physical death; and the Star shows the transmigration of souls that occurs between death and incarnation. The wings of the Kerubim form a vesica that encloses the universe, an indication that all manifestation is governed by the cycle of birth, life, death, and afterlife.

Interpretation

In a reading, the Universe signifies the full manifestation and completion of a situation or a project. It may also indicate that it is time to finish what you have started. The Maiden dominates the serpent, which signifies the power of the will to manifest results and achieve material goals. The Kerubim symbolize the practical use of knowledge and learning to take control of life and determine your own destiny.

The Universe reversed indicates a failure to bring completion and closure to a situation. You may have run out of time or resources to finish what you've started. The serpent dominates the Maiden, suggesting the restriction of Saturn and slavery to materialistic desires. This reversed trump may also signify reluctance to recognize that a situation has ended—a refusal to let go, give up, and move on.

2

The Court Cards

The symbolism of the court cards is based on an elemental and astrological framework presented in *Book T*. The Knight, Queen, Prince, and Princess correspond with the four letters of the Tetragrammaton. The elemental attributions of the Tetragrammaton combined with those of the four suits form the sixteen sub-elements that make up the elemental attribution of each court card. See page 188 for a table listing the attributions of the court cards.

The zodiacal attributions of the court cards are specified in *Book T*, which assigns three decans of the zodiac (30°) to the Knight, Queen, and Prince cards. Each card is assigned the last decan of one sign and the first two decans of the following sign. The Princess cards rule one quarter of the zodiacal wheel (three signs or 60°). Their zodiacal quarters are centered on the kerubic signs that match their respective suits.

The crests and symbols are derived from a chart of the special characteristics of the court cards found in *Book T*.[51] Many of the crests are symbols of the zodiacal attributions of the court cards.

In a tarot reading, court cards usually represent people who are influential in the querent's situation. A list of personality traits has been given to help the reader identify the person in question, and also to signify how that person may behave in the situation described in the reading.

In the Thoth deck, each court card also illustrates a key concept that may be pertinent to the subject of the reading. For example, the King of Wands indicates the initiation of a new project, while the Princess of Wands signifies independence and nonconformity. The interpretation of court cards is discussed in more detail in chapter 4.

Wands

The suit of Wands represents the element of Fire, the creative and energetic realm represented by the flames present in each card. The salient (straight) flames represent feminine energy and the waved flames represent masculine energy.[52]

In the Knight of Wands, the flames are waved, while in the Queen the flames are salient. *Book T* dictates that the Prince of Wands should be set in both waved and salient flames to represent the energy of both Knight and Queen; Crowley has ignored this detail, using the feminine salient flames to balance out the dominant masculine symbolism in the Prince. The Princess of Wands ascends on leaping, waved flames, while salient flames burn upon her altar and radiate from her wand.

---

51.   Regardie, *The Golden Dawn*, 551.
52.   Ibid., 175.

Description

The Knight of Wands represents Fire of Fire, showing Fire's activity and energy. His crest is a black horse, which is attributed to Mars, the ruler of Scorpio.

The flaming club is a relative of the Ace of Wands, projecting out from the Knight's groin like a phallus. In support of this sexual interpretation, the yellow and white rays in the background roughly converge in the Knight's navel chakra, which is associated with sexual pleasure. In this sexual context, Fire of Fire can be reinterpreted as Yod of Yod, the active sperm; yet also remember that the Knights represent "a force swift and violent in action, but whose effect soon passes away."[53]

The background is bright pale yellow, the color of the Fool in Atziluth. Like the Fool, the Knight of Wands initiates the series of cards to which it belongs. The winds are at his back, blowing hair, beard, mane, and tail forward and upward as he charges upon the flames.

Personality Traits

Active, aggressive, angry, assertive, competitive, confident, dynamic, impulsive, initiating, irritable, narrow-minded, pioneering, short-tempered, violent. A leader.

Knight of Wands

Elemental Attribution
Fire of Fire

Zodiacal Attribution
20° Scorpio—20° Sagittarius

Crest
Winged black horse's head

Symbols
Black horse, waving flames, flaming club like Ace, scarlet cloak

Key Concept
The initiation of a new project

Knight of Wands

---

53. Regardie, *The Golden Dawn*, 544.

Queen of Wands

Elemental Attribution
Water of Fire

Zodiacal Attribution
20˚ Pisces–20˚ Aries

Crest
Winged leopard's head

Symbols
Leopard,
steady flames,
Thyrsus Wand

Key Concept
Control over one's self
or others

Queen of Wands

Description

Twelve rays of light emanate from the crown of the Queen of Wands, the number of signs in the zodiac. The zodiac in turn is a representation of Nuit, the omnipresent Mother.[54] The outline of the Queen's crown and her bosom form a vesica, another maternal symbol.

In her left hand, the Queen holds a wand crowned with a pinecone. This wand is the Thyrsus, the symbol and weapon of the Maenads of Greek myth. The Maenads (Greek for "mad women") were the followers of Dionysus or Bacchus (the Latin name of Dionysus), and they were characterized as having unbridled lust and animalistic passions. The wand crosses her navel chakra and the groin of the leopard. The wand resembles a phallus, suggesting that she is a "woman satisfied."[55]

Her right hand rests on the head of a leopard. The leopard symbolizes the Nephesch or animal soul, the primal urges and drives also signified by the Thyrsus. Her hand upon the head of the leopard indicates that she is in control of the animal passions and desires of the Nephesch.

Personality Traits

Altruistic, controlling, commanding, detached, frank, honest, idealistic, impatient, impressionable, loyal, restless.

---

54. See the descriptions of the Empress and the Sun.
55. See the description of Adjustment.

Description

The Prince of Wands wears a crown of eleven rays, the number of magick. He holds a Phoenix Wand in his right hand, which is the Wand of the Second Adept (Adeptus Major 6=5) in the Adeptus Minor ceremony of the Golden Dawn.[56] The Phoenix Wand is red with a green eye and foot, the flashing colors of Fire. The chariot is also painted in the flashing colors of red and green. Draped over his left wrist are the reins of the lion, red to signify his passion, as indicated in the Lust card. The lion that draws his chariot is Leo, the kerubic sign attributed to this card.

The most unusual symbol in this card is the sigil of To Mega Therion, composed of the Mark of the Beast conjoined with the seven-pointed Star of Babalon. This was obviously Crowley's personal court card, so chosen on the basis that Leo was his ascendant, and also probably on the association of Leo with the Lust card. Crowley even goes so far as to take the name Leo as his pseudonym in "The Master Therion: A Biographical Note" in *The Heart of the Master*.[57]

The character that Crowley describes in *The Book of Thoth* is none other than himself, which is why he expounds upon the nature of this character at greater length than the other court cards. As if to emphasize this important relationship, the Prince of Wands is one of the two court card figures drawn with pupils in

---

56. See the Five of Wands for comparison.
57. Crowley, Aleister, *The Heart of the Master* (Tempe, AZ: New Falcon, 1992), 11–21.

Prince of Wands

Elemental Attribution
Air of Fire

Zodiacal Attribution
20° Cancer–20° Leo

Crest
Winged lion's head

Symbols
Lion, salient flames,
Fire Wand of Zelator Adept

Key Concept
The need for recognition

Prince of Wands

their eyes. (The other figure with pupils is the Queen of Swords, who represents the first two decans of Libra, Crowley's Sun sign.)

The Prince rides upon salient flames, not waved and salient flames. The exclusive use of feminine flames in this card may constitute an effort to balance the active, masculine elemental attribution of Fire of Air.

Personality Traits

Ambitious, attention-seeking, attractive, bold, charismatic, dramatic, egotistical, generous, noble, pompous, proud, self-confident, strong.

Description

The Princess of Wands wears a crown of two stylized ostrich plumes, the crown of Maat, signifying justice and identifying her with the Daughter of Adjustment. The tiger's head crest of *Book T* has become an actual tiger. The tiger is attributed to Leo, and it is amber in color, Cancer in Atziluth; both signs are attributed to this card.

In her left hand she holds a Sun Wand of thirty rays, a reference to the path of Resh and the Sun trump. Dashed rays radiate from the salient flames of the Sun disk, indicative of the fiery feminine impulse of this card. The altar is the gold of the Sun, and is adorned with rams' heads, the glyph of Aries. Aries is the herald of spring, and when the Sun enters Aries at the Spring Equinox the hours of daylight and darkness are equal. This is symbolized by the two bands of rams' heads around the altar, one inverted and one upright, with twelve heads in each row. Burning upon the altar of Spring are five roses, representative of passion of the five senses.

The Princess of Wands represents the Earthy part of Fire, but there is no earth upon which to stand in this card. The flame behind her is shaped like the letter Yod, which is associated not only with Fire but also Virgo, another astrological attribution of this card. The greenish tint of the flames alludes to Virgo in Atziluth and the element of Earth.

Personality Traits

Avenging, daring, freedom-loving, impulsive, independent, irrational, nonconforming, temperamental, unruly, unstable.

Princess of Wands

Elemental Attribution
Earth of Fire

Zodiacal Attribution
Cancer, Leo, Virgo

Crest
Ostrich plumes

Symbols
Tiger, leaping flames, gold altar, Sun Wand

Key Concepts
Nonconformity and independence

Princess of Wands

Cups

The suit of Cups represents the element of Water, the emotional and intuitive realm. The bodies of water present in each of these court cards represent the different emotional states illustrated therein. See table 4.

Table 4: Bodies of water and their meanings

Court Card	Body of Water	Emotional States
Knight of Cups	Sea	Expression and transcendence
Queen of Cups	Pool	Reflection and empathy
Prince of Cups	Lake	Repression and rationalization
Princess of Cups	Sea with spray	Fantasy and imagination

Description

The armor of the Knight of Cups is olive, the mixture of the green of Netzach and the violet of the Yesod found in the saltire of Malkuth. The traditional path between Netzach and Yesod is that of Aquarius, one of the zodiacal attributions of this card.

The Knight holds a cup of russet, the mixture of the orange of Hod and the violet of Yesod. The colors of russet and olive are on opposite quarters of the saltire of Malkuth; together they represent the elements of Fire and Water, the elemental attribution of this card.

From the cup issues a crab, the symbol of Cancer. The crab is amber, Cancer in Atziluth. Behind the crab are nine waves or rays, showing the influence of the Moon, the planetary ruler of Cancer that directs the tides of the seas and oceans.

The Knight of Cups is the only court figure that does not wear a helmet. The peacock crest of *Book T* has become a peacock at the bottom of the card. The peacock is a glyph heralding the end of the Nigredo, or blackening stage of alchemical work, and the transmutation of the First Matter into a more spiritualized form. Thus the Knight is winged to signify his purified state, and his white horse (the color of the Albedo, the next stage of alchemy) leaps over the peacock to illustrate this important change. The colorful plumage of the peacock also suggests the florescence and brilliance of Water in its Fiery aspect.

Personality Traits

Emotional, empathic, moody, hypersensitive, nurturing, overcautious, paternal, protective, romantic, supportive, tenacious.

Knight of Cups

Elemental Attribution
Fire of Water

Zodiacal Attribution
20° Aquarius—20° Pisces

Crest
None

Symbols
White horse,
crab issuing from cup,
peacock, sea

Key Concepts
Aspiration; looking toward
the future

Knight of Cups

Queen of Cups

Elemental Attribution
Water of Water

Zodiacal Attribution
20° Gemini—20° Cancer

Crest
Ibis

Symbols
Ibis, crayfish issuing from cup, lotus, pool

Key Concept
The emotions controlling the intellect

Queen of Cups

Description

The Queen of Cups represents the receptive and reflective powers of the element of Water in affinity with the symbol of the Moon. The Moon rises above and behind the Queen, and the curves of light that veil her are the currents of the Astral Light of Yesod. The shell that she holds in her left hand is a symbol not only of the life of the Waters but also of the womb, which is an attribution of both Yesod and the Moon. The reflection of the Queen in the waters below shows the Moon emanating from the shell-cup itself, which strengthens the connection between the two symbols.

The crayfish is a symbol from the Moon card, where it is representative of the most basic level of consciousness (the Nephesch) from which our primal emotions originate. It also alludes to the astrological attribution of the Queen, as indicated in the Philosophus Ritual of the Golden Dawn:

> The Crayfish is the sign Cancer and was anciently the Scarabeus or Khephera, the emblem of the Sun below the Horizon as he ever is when the Moon is increasing above. Also, when the Sun is in the sign Pisces the Moon will be well in her increase in Cancer as shown by the Crayfish emblem.[58]

The Queen holds a lotus on her right hand, which rests upon the head of an ibis. The lotus is a key symbol of the suit of Cups, and represents not only Water but also the emotions. The lotus has nine

---

58. Regardie, *The Golden Dawn*, 185.

88

petals, connecting it with Yesod and the Moon. The ibis is a symbol of Thoth, an Egyptian Moon god. Associated with the Sephira Hod, Thoth is also a symbol of the intellect. Together these symbols illustrate the key concept of the emotions overriding and controlling the intellect.

The pool below the Queen emphasizes the distortional quality of Water and the emotions. The two lotuses floating on the placid waters allude to the attribution of Gemini to this card. There are a total of three lotuses in this card, the number of Binah, the Great Sea and womb of all life.

Personality Traits

Calm, compassionate, emotional, inattentive, intuitive, maternal, observant, passive, receptive, sensitive, spiritual, sympathetic, understanding, unrealistic, unreliable.

Prince of Cups

Elemental Attribution
Air of Water

Zodiacal Attribution
20° Libra–20° Scorpio

Crest
Eagle

Symbols
Eagle, serpent issuing from cup, lotus, lake

Key Concept
The intellect controlling the emotions

Prince of Cups

Description

The Prince of Cups is naked except for his crested helm. His skin is blue-green, the color of Scorpio in Atziluth. The eagle that draws his chariot represents the highest form of the alchemical Scorpio, which is discussed at length in the description of the Death trump. The black reins in his left hand suggest the process of putrefaction, also associated with Scorpio.

He holds a cup in his left hand, and from this cup issues a coiling serpent, the second form of the alchemical Scorpio. The serpent is also a symbol of Mercury and the intellect. White vapor or steam (Air of Water) rises from the cup.

In his right hand the Prince holds a lotus, inverted to signify the rejection of the intuitive or emotional realm, while he gazes intently into the cup at the serpent symbolic of Mercury. This card signifies the intellect dominating intuition; compare it with the Queen of Cups.

The number eight occurs frequently in the feather groupings of the eagle. Eight is associated with Hod and Mercury, while the eagle is the kerubic symbol of Water. As a whole, the eagle is therefore a symbol of the Air of Water attribution of this card. Behind the Prince are eight wisps of vapor (Air of Water), and below him rain falls on a lake.

Personality Traits

Compulsive, focused, intense, introverted, irritable, jealous, magnetic, passionate, passive-aggressive, secretive, skeptical, willful.

Description

The swan crest of the Princess of Cups is attributed to Venus, the ruler of Libra. Ten rays extend out from the crest, the number of Malkuth and Earth. The ice or salt crystals on her crest and her dress reflect her attribution of Earth of Water. The crystals on her dress are hexagonal, indicating the balance of Tiphareth, and they are eleven in number, the number of magick.

In her right hand she bears a shell-like cup containing a turtle, an attribution of Cancer. In her left hand she holds a lotus, held upright to symbolize her acceptance and expression of the emotional realm. Her skin, the cup, and the turtle are green, the color of Earth.

The dolphin is attributed to Pisces in Crowley's *777*, and therefore it signifies the influence of the Queen of Cups, the mother of the Princess. (Likewise, the turtle of Cancer shows the influence of her father, the King of Cups.) The dolphin is also traditionally a symbol of Venus, and the four points of its pectoral fin link it with the Empress, the trump attributed to Venus. Overall, the dolphin is symbolic of the feminine creative principle.[59]

Personality Traits

Accepting, childish, emotionally unstable, gracious, graceful, imaginative, intuitive, loving, social, unrealistic.

---

59. See the Two of Cups description for a more detailed analysis of the dolphin.

Princess of Cups

Elemental Attribution
Earth of Water

Zodiacal Attribution
Libra, Scorpio, Sagittarius

Crest
Swan

Symbols
Dolphin, turtle issuing from cup, lotus, sea with ice crystals

Key Concepts
Dreams and fantasy

Princess of Cups

Swords

The suit of Swords represents the element of Air, the mental or intellectual realm. Aspects of the mind are symbolized by the different cloud formations found in each court card of the suit (see table 5).

Table 5: Cloud formations and their meaning

Court Card	Cloud Formation	Description	Meaning
Knight of Swords	Dark stratus	Flat, horizontal	Direction, focus of mind
Queen of Swords	Gray cumulus	Heaped	Accumulation of ideas
Prince of Swords	Gray nimbus	Diffused	Diffusion of mind
Princess of Swords	White clouds (all formations)	(All)	Synthesis of mental processes

Furthermore, the four court cards of the suit of Swords correspond with the Qabalistic parts of the soul through mutual attributions to the Sephiroth (see table 6).

Table 6: Court cards of Swords and their Qabalistic Parts of the Soul correspondences.

Court Card	Sephira	Part of Soul
Knight of Swords	Chokmah	Chiah
Queen of Swords	Binah	Neschamah
Prince of Swords	Tiphareth	Ruach
Princess of Swords	Malkuth	Nephesch

Each of the court cards bears symbolism that connects it with the appropriate Sephira. The Knight of Swords shows three swallows, birds attributed to Beth and Mercury. Beth connects the Yechidah and the Chiah, and Chokmah is the higher octave of Mercury. The Chiah is the will or creative impulse of the soul, and the Knight rides with the focus and determination characteristic of that impulse.

The Queen of Swords has for a crest a child's head "like the head of an infantile Kerub, seen sculptored on tombs."[60] This association with tombs links the crest to Saturn and Binah. The Neschamah is the aspiration and intuition of the soul. The

---

60. Regardie, *The Golden Dawn*, 548.

card shows the Queen holding a severed head, representative of the ego, or Ruach, and crowned with the child's head representative of the Neschamah.

The Prince of Swords is connected with the Ruach, the intellect or ego of the soul. The card shows the Prince with sword upraised as if to sever his connection with the fairies that pull his chariot (the mind) haphazardly in every direction. It is through this act that he comes to the realization of the Neschamah, symbolized by the child's head crest.

Finally, the Princess of Swords is connected to the Nephesch through her crest, the head of Medusa. The Nephesch is the animal soul, the primal emotions and sensations of the soul. The head of a woman with serpents for hair is symbolic of the reptilian brain responsible for the primal impulses of the Nephesch. On the card the Princess assumes a defensive, reactive stance like a cornered animal. She stabs downward with her sword as if to plunge it into the rising Sun, representative of the Ruach.

Knight of Swords

Elemental Attribution
Fire of Air

Zodiacal Attribution
20° Taurus—20° Gemini

Crest
Winged hexagram

Symbols
Yellow horse, stratus clouds, drawn sword and poniard

Key Concept
Attack: taking advantage of opportunity

Knight of Swords

Description

The Knight of Swords wears citrine armor, the color of Air in Malkuth, and his horse is drawn in russet, the color of Fire in Malkuth. Together they signify the elemental attribution of this card, Fire of Air. His crest is a six-pointed star that extends into four wings bearing the names of the four directions. The Knight is leaping to the southeast, and if he is oriented with the elemental attributions of the quarters as presented in the Lesser Banishing Ritual of the Pentagram, he rides between Fire and Air.

The Knight holds a sword with a winged guard in his right hand, the wings suggestive of the element of Air. In his left hand is a poniard, a type of dagger with a slender blade used for stabbing as opposed to cutting. The guard forms the sigil of the Sun, which is associated with Fire. Thus the sword and poniard together also signify the attribution of Fire of Air.

The swallows that fly alongside the Knight are attributed to Mercury, the ruler of Gemini. The influence of Gemini is also indicated by the two blades and the winged hexagram, which is attributed to Castor and Pollux in *Book T*.[61]

Personality Traits

Ambiguous, compromising, cooperative, detached, impartial, inconsistent, indecisive, impatient, persuasive, tactful, tolerant.

---

61. Regardie, *The Golden Dawn*, 548.

Description

The Queen of Swords wears a helm adorned with a child's head "like the head of an infantile Kerub, seen sculptored on tombs."[62] The association with tombs links it to Saturn, who is exalted in Libra, an astrological attribution of this card. Also, the Egyptians associated Libra with the god Khonsu, a Moon god depicted as a child whose image appears above the scales in the zodiac of Dendera. Crowley's Sun sign is Libra, and therefore the Queen is one of the two court cards drawn with pupils in the eyes. (The other card with pupils is the Prince of Wands.) Fifteen rays radiate from the Queen's crest, the numeration of Hod spelled out in full; Mercury is the ruler of Virgo, the other astrological attribution of this card.

She holds a sword in her left hand and a severed, bearded head in her right hand. The sword signifies analysis, and the bearded head represents old ideas and old ways of thinking. The child's head crest represents the new ideas taking the place of the old. It is in this context that she is "the Liberator of the Mind."[63]

Personality Traits

Analytical, cold, communicative, curious, intelligent, logical, open-minded, quick-thinking, unreliable, witty.

Queen of Swords

Elemental Attribution
Water of Air

Zodiacal Attribution
20° Virgo—20° Libra

Crest
Child's head

Symbols
Head of an old man severed, cumulus clouds, drawn sword

Key Concepts
Letting go of old ideas and grasping new ideas

Queen of Swords

---

62. Regardie, *The Golden Dawn*, 548.
63. Crowley, *The Book of Thoth*, 161.

Prince of Swords

Elemental Attribution
Air of Air

Zodiacal Attribution
20° Capricorn–20° Aquarius

Crest
Child's head

Symbols
Winged fairies, nimbus clouds, drawn sword and sickle

Key Concepts
Thought without action; plans unrealized

Prince of Swords

Description

The Prince of Swords wears a helm of gold, the color of the Sun and Tiphareth. The child's head crest is a symbol of the Ruach, the child also being an attribution of Tiphareth.

In his left hand, the Prince grasps a sickle and the reins of his chariot, and in his right hand is a sword upraised as if to strike. The sword creates and analyzes ideas, while the sickle (the weapon of Saturn) destroys them. The Air of Air attribution makes the Prince purely intellectual, full of ideas but unable to manifest them before they are lost. It is only by learning to control the ego (Ruach) that the Prince can sever his connection with the fairies (thoughts) that pull his chariot in random and conflicting directions.

The fairies in this card are degradations of man as the Kerub of Air, attributed to Aquarius. The wings of the Prince and fairies, and parts of the chariot are yellow, the color of Air. The bodies of the Prince and fairies are blue emerald green, the color of Aleph (Air) in Yetzirah (Air), or simply Air of Air. On the front of his chariot is a yellow diamond within a dark green disk. The diamond is a symbol of Air; it has eight sides, suggesting Hod, Mercury, and the intellect.

Personality Traits

Extremist, freedom-loving, humanitarian, individualistic, imaginative, intellectual, intelligent, inventive, scatterbrained, superficial, tolerant, unfocused.

Description

The crest of the Princess of Swords is the Medusa's head, the Aegis of Minerva, who is associated with this card in *Book T* and is the goddess attributed to Aquarius in *777*. The Princess wears the winged sandals of Mercury, the planet exalted in Aquarius. The winged sandals also appear in the myth of Perseus, who used them on his quest to obtain the head of Medusa. The Princess is painted in the colors of Air: her scarf is yellow, her tunic is sky blue, and her body is emerald and yellow.

The Princess stabs downward with the sword of analysis, imitating her mother the Queen. Her left hand rests upon a silver altar with gray smoke rising from it. Smoke is the Earthy part of Air, an elemental attribution also symbolized by the design on the altar of disks (Earth) over diamonds (Air).

She stands upon cumulus clouds of the Queen of Swords, and in the background are the stratus clouds of the Knight of Swords. Before her is an archway through which the rising Sun appears. The Sun is Tiphareth, the Ruach, and the Princess of Swords (representative of the Nephesch) holds the sword as if to defend herself from its awesome power.

Personality Traits

Argumentative, cautious, crafty, defensive, fearful, instinctive, judgmental, reactive, self-preserving.

Princess of Swords

Elemental Attribution
Earth of Air

Zodiacal Attribution
Capricorn, Aquarius, Pisces

Crest
Medusa's head

Symbols
Silver altar, smoke, clouds, drawn sword

Key Concept
Defense

Princess of Swords

Disks

The suit of Disks represents the element of Earth, the material and financial realm. In *Book T*, the backgrounds of the four court cards of the suit are representative of the four seasons (see table 7).

Table 7: Court cards of Disks and their background correspondences

Court card	Background	Season
Knight of Disks	Cultivated land	Autumn
Queen of Disks	Desert	Summer
Prince of Disks	Flowery land	Spring
Princess of Disks	Grove of bare trees	Winter

The Knight of Disks stands among cultivated fields and wheat, and he carries a flail for threshing wheat, all indicating autumn, the time of the harvest. The background of the Queen shows a desert with oases, suggestive of the summer heat, and the Queen is African in appearance. The Prince rides among the flowers and leaved plants that burst into color in the spring. The background of the Princess of Disks is a grove of bare trees, suggestive of winter. Furthermore, the Princess has a Nordic or Celtic appearance, and she wears a heavy mantle of sheepskin that would be proper for the winter months.

Description:

The Knight of Disks continues and completes the color symbolism found throughout the knights, wearing a russet cloak over black armor, the color of Fire and Earth in Malkuth. The red saddle and black shield also bear out this elemental attribution.

The suit symbol has been transformed into a shield in accordance with the aggressive nature of the knights. The face of the shield-disk is hidden, but it is probable that it is the pentacle of the Zelator Adeptus Minor of traditional design (see figure 5). This pentacle consists of the saltire of Malkuth in Briah over which is painted a hexagram, the symbol of the Sun that here visibly radiates light upon the cultivated land. This light is tinted yellow, amber, and rose—all solar colors. The visible side of the shield bears the symbols of Fire and Earth incorporated into its design. It is black, not only because of its attribution to Earth but also in contrast to the light that radiates from its face.

Figure 5. The Pentacle of the Zelator Adeptus Minor

Knight of Disks

Elemental Attribution
Fire of Earth

Zodiacal Attribution
20° Leo—20° Virgo

Crest
Stag's head

Symbols
Brown horse, cultivated land, flail, pentacle as Zelator Adept

Key Concept
Realization of plans

Knight of Disks

His crest is a winged stag's head, and the stag was associated with the cardinal virtue of prudence during the Renaissance. This virtue is also attributed to the Hermit and Virgo, which is an astrological attribution of this card. The Knight rests in a field of ripened wheat, also found in the Hermit. The wooden flail he holds has been used to thresh wheat since ancient times. This links the flail with Virgo, the sign associated with fertility and the harvest.

Personality Traits

Analytical, constructive, critical, discriminating, humble, orderly, perfectionistic, practical, pragmatic, tedious, thrifty, unsympathetic.

Description

The Queen of Disks gazes upon the desert behind her; she is the only Queen in the deck who does not face forward. Instead of the traditional crest of the goat's head, Crowley has substituted the horns of the markhor, a wild goat found in mountainous regions from Afghanistan to India, possibly an animal he encountered in his travels in that region. On the other hand, *markhor* means "snake eater," an obvious reference to oral sex, and horns are symbols of masculine energy and virility.

In her right hand the Queen bears a long wand crowned with a hexagram inside a cube. This wand is a combination of the traditional wands of the King and Queen of Disks. The hexagram is a symbol of the Sun and the cube signifies the Earth; therefore, the wand symbolizes the fertility of the Earth as engendered by the Sun.

In her left arm she cradles a golden orb of thirteen interlocking rings. The orb is the Sun, and the 13th path is the Priestess and the Moon, which is complementary to the element of Water and reflects the light of the Sun. Thus the orb represents passivity (the Moon) expressed in its highest aspect (the Sun).

A goat stands on a second golden orb in the foreground, which represents the Sun in Capricorn, a zodiacal attribution of this card. Capricorn as the Devil represents masculine creative energy, a fitting complement to the fertile nature of the Queen of Disks. Behind the Queen is a desert with oases and a river weaving through it, symbolic of Water of Earth.

Queen of Disks

Elemental Attribution
Water of Earth

Zodiacal Attribution
20° Sagittarius—
20° Capricorn

Crest
Markhor (goat) horns

Symbols
Desert, goat, scepter with cube, orb of gold

Key Concept
Looking into the past

Queen of Disks

Personality Traits

Ambitious, cautious, conservative, determined, fertile, industrious, solitary, materialistic, reserved, serious, uncompromising, virile.

Description

The winged bull's head crest of the Prince signifies Taurus, the kerubic attribution of this card. In his right hand he bears a scepter crowned with an orb and cross, a symbol of dominion over the Earth. The Prince and the bull that draws his chariot are red-orange, the color of Taurus in Atziluth. The chariot is black, the color of Earth.

The disk in his left hand is traditionally an orb of gold. Crowley has elaborated on the symbol by adding a cross, a cube, and three circles. The golden orb is a symbol of the Sun, and the cross and cube are symbols of Earth; together they symbolize the life-giving energy of the Sun and its role in agriculture. The orb is held downward to emphasize the Prince's role and control over this process.

Globules of nitrogen line the canopy of the chariot, gas (Air) fixated in the soil (Earth). In the background, flowers and vegetation flourish in the fertile earth.

Personality Traits

Dependable, gentle, hardworking, materialistic, patient, possessive, self-indulgent, sensual, slow-moving, stable, steady, stubborn.

Prince of Disks

Elemental Attribution
Air of Earth

Zodiacal Attribution
20° Aries—20° Taurus

Crest
Winged bull's head

Symbols
Flowery land, bull, scepter with orb and cross, orb held downward

Key Concepts
Growth and management

Prince of Disks

Princess of Disks

Elemental Attribution
Earth of Earth

Zodiacal Attribution
Aries, Taurus, Gemini

Crest
Ram's head

Symbols
Grove of bare trees, scepter
with diamond, pentacle,
wheat-sheaf altar

Key Concepts
Completion and renewal

Princess of Disks

Description

The Princess is crowned with a ram's head, a glyph of Aries, one of the astrological attributions of this card. She is cloaked in sheepskin, also alluding to Aries. Her gown is sheer and reveals her to be pregnant. Thus the Princess is the Daughter who has become the Mother; she renews the cycle of the Tetragrammaton.

In her right hand she bears a scepter or spear with a diamond head, inverted and emitting rays of light. The illuminating diamond of Kether is symbolic of the beginning of the cycle of the court cards. The bright pale yellow light (of the Fool in Atziluth) emitted from the spear appears in the background of the King of Wands, who bears a flaming club reminiscent of the Ace of Wands (Kether in Atziluth).

In her left hand the Princess holds a pentacle painted in the same solar colors as the Ace of Pentacles: rose, yellow, salmon, and amber. The yin-yang symbol in the center of the rose is surrounded by three bands of twelve petals. The petals represent the thirty-six decans that make up the solar year, which begins in Aries.

The Princess stands in a grove of leafless trees; the ground is transparent to show the trees' roots, which, like the rest of the scene, are lit from below. The background is painted in the orange and yellow of Gemini and the brown of Taurus. Beside her is a stone altar with sheaves of wheat carved into it. The wheat sheaf is sacred to Demeter, goddess of the Earth and the mother that renews the cycle of the court cards. The Princess symbolizes the renewal of the Earth that comes after the cold winter.

Personality Traits

Confident, enduring, inflexible, persistent, practical, premeditative, self-disciplined, sensual, stable.

$$\boxed{3}$$

The Suit Cards

The suit cards of tarot decks published before the twentieth century were usually very simple, showing only the symbol of the suit laid out in a symmetrical pattern. This changed with the publication of the Rider-Waite tarot deck, when Pamela Colman Smith painted each of the suit cards with medieval-style scenes that illustrated their meanings. It is this conception of the suit cards that is the most common in modern tarot decks.

The suit cards of the Thoth deck offer a unique compromise between the old and new styles. The illustrative scenes have been eschewed in favor of suit cards modeled after the pip design of the medieval decks. At the same time, more complicated symbolism and color have been added to bring greater depth and meaning to the images.

Three primary attributions determine the general symbolism of the suit cards: the suit elements, the Qabalistic attributions of a Sephira in one of the Four Worlds, and the astrological attributions of a planet in a sign (see the appendix for the full table). In the case of the four aces, the astrological attribution is replaced by the attribution of a letter of the Tetragrammaton assigned according to suit.

Each suit card is given a title derived from *Book T*. The title indicates the general meaning of the card, and is printed on the card to assist the tarot reader with interpretation.

Description

A large wand is marked with the Tree of Life. Ten Yods of flame form the Sephiroth, and the twenty-two paths are carved into the wood. Eighteen green lightning bolts shoot out from the wand, symbolic of unbridled and uncontained creative force. Eighteen is the numeration of *chai*, Hebrew for "living." The wand also represents an erect phallus, and the Yods signify the ejaculated sperm.[64] The background and the lightning are painted in the flashing colors of Fire: red and green.

Interpretation

Energy. Strength. The creative impulse. Natural force as opposed to invoked force. Compare this card with the Ace of Swords.

Reversed

Suggests that the means of realizing the well-dignified interpretations are blocked in a way that may be defined by the surrounding cards.

Ace of Wands

Title
The Root of the
Powers of Fire

Qabalistic Attribution
Kether in Atziluth

Tetragrammaton Attribution
Yod

---

64.   See the description of the Hermit.

Two of Wands

Title
Dominion

Qabalistic Attribution
Chokmah in Atziluth

Astrological Attribution
Mars in Aries

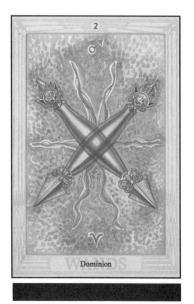

Description

The two wands are Dorjes crossed. Crowley defines the Dorje as "the Tibetan symbol of the thunderbolt, the emblem of celestial Power, but more in its destructive than its creative form."[65] The six flames represent the energy of the Sun (Tiphareth), which combined with the fiery planet Mars and the fiery sign Aries (ruled by Mars) is symbolic of tremendous force. This card represents the destruction of total freedom in order to direct or control energy or force.

The blue background of this card approximates that of Chokmah in Atziluth, pure soft blue. The fiery energy of Mars and Aries disperses the cloudiness and confusion of the mind, revealing the blue sky of clarity.

Interpretation

Dominion (domain, supreme authority). Power. Influence over another. Harnessing and controlling the direction of energy or force.

Reversed

Dictatorship. Revenge. Obstinacy. Turbulence.

---

65. Crowley, *The Book of Thoth*, 189.

Description

Three Lotus Wands are crossed, and ten straight and ten curved flames issue from their junction. Six of the straight flames are white, representing the balancing influence of the Sun. The golden shafts of the wands also suggest the Sun. The remaining flames symbolize the energy of the previous two cards: the ten curvy flames represent the ten Sephiroth found in the Ace of Wands, while the four straight flames of orange suggest the Dorjes crossed in the Two of Wands.

The energy of the previous two cards has become manifest in Binah. The concept of birth or creation is also found in the astrological attribution of Sun in Aries. The Sun is exalted in Aries, and Aries marks the beginning of spring.

The Lotus Wand is associated with Isis, the Great Mother of the Egyptians, and symbolizes the power of creation. Each lotus has nine petals, linking them with the creative and watery Sephira Yesod. At the same time, the Lotus Wand is the magickal weapon of Tiphareth in the Adeptus Minor Ritual of the Golden Dawn. Thus the idea of creation is everywhere implicit.

As a final note, the figures in this card are outlined in crimson, the color of Binah in Atziluth.

Interpretation

Creation. Birth. Established strength. Success of initial struggle. Realization of hope. Possibly pride, nobility, or power.

Reversed

Conceit (too much pride). Arrogance. Delusions of grandeur, strength, or accomplishment.

Three of Wands

Title
Virtue

Qabalistic Attribution
Binah in Atziluth

Astrological Attribution
Sun in Aries

Four of Wands

Title
Completion

Qabalistic Attribution
Chesed in Atziluth

Astrological Attribution
Venus in Aries

Description

The four wands are arranged in a circle. Each wand is adorned with the ram of Aries (representing energy of will) and the dove of Venus (representing love). The circle represents the limitation or completion of work.

The wands cross to form an eight-rayed star, and eight flames issue out from the center. Eight is the numeration of the Hebrew words *abah* ("to will") *ahab* ("to love"), and *ahgad* ("to bind or collect"), all signifying key ideas associated with this card. "Love Is the Law, Love under Will" (AL I:57).

The astrological sigils are drawn in the red of Aries, and the background is tinted the green of Venus. Red and green are also the flashing colors of Fire.

Interpretation

Completion, usually of a labor of love and will. It may mean conclusion or rest after labor, depending on the situation and surrounding cards.

Reversed

A labor forced or undesired. The expansiveness of Jupiter in Chesed may take over, suggesting a monumental labor far from completion and possibly overwhelming. A labor rushed due to anxiety that is not complete because of unreliability, imbalance, or unreadiness. A labor complete but unstable.

Description

The Five of Wands uses the Adept's wands from the Adeptus Minor Ritual of the Golden Dawn as symbols.[66] The smaller wands are disordered and elementally discordant in nature. The Lotus Wands have shafts of blue that concur with their attribution to Water, but the heads of the wands are purple, the mixture of red (Fire) and blue (Water). The shafts of the Phoenix Wands are the orange of Geburah in Atziluth, but the heads of the wands are the blue of Water. Furthermore, the Phoenix Wands face the Lotus Wands (as opposed to their arrangement in subsequent cards) as if the pairs are in conflict or discord.

The caduceus dominates the other wands. The caduceus is the Wand of the Chief Adept, attributed to Chesed, and thus the shaft is blue and the wings are four in number. This wand also signifies the authority of Jupiter. The wings on the base and top of the wand are purple, the mixture of Fire and Water. The serpents symbolize the unification of opposing forces, and they wear the crowns of Upper and Lower Egypt, the two lands that merged to become the vast and mighty Egyptian empire.

The most interesting aspect of this card is the seal on the caduceus—the Mark of the Beast conjoined with the Star of Babalon, the phallus inside the womb. As with the serpents and the wings, this is a symbol of the conjunction of positive and negative energy, of male and female, and of Fire and Water. Remember also that the caduceus, as the

---

66. The Adeptus Minor Ritual may be found in Regardie's *The Golden Dawn*, 221–247.

Five of Wands

Title
Strife

Qabalistic Attribution
Geburah in Atziluth

Astrological Attribution
Saturn in Leo

Wand of Mercury, is also attributed to the element of Air, the child of the union of Fire and Water.

The Mark of the Beast is drawn in blue upon an orange background, the flashing colors of Water, reflecting the watery nature of Chesed and further identifying the wand with Jupiter's authority.

The sigils of Saturn and Leo appear in red upon the shaft of the caduceus. The Fire of Leo is smothered by the serious and restrictive nature of Saturn. Saturn also conflicts with the planetary attributions of this card, opposing the swiftness of Mercury (the caduceus) and the expansiveness of Jupiter (Chesed).

Ten flames leap from the junction of the wands. This is a reference to the Ten of Wands, which demonstrates what occurs when Saturn is allowed to completely dominate the Fire of the suit of Wands. It is due to the fiery nature of Geburah and the authority of the caduceus that this card is titled "Strife" and not "Oppression."[67]

Interpretation
Strife. Quarreling. Fighting. Conflict. Competition. Possibly violence.

Reversed
Prodigality or generosity.

---

67. "Oppression" is the title of the Ten of Wands.

Description

The six Adepts' wands are balanced and paired, indicative of the harmony of Tiphareth. The lotuses are blue and white, the colors of Water and Spirit. The Phoenix heads are the yellow of Tiphareth. The solar disk of the caduceus is red and the wings are blue, signifying the union of opposites (Fire and Water) as the power of this wand.

The shafts of the wands are reddish amber, the color of Leo in the Assiah. Everywhere the strength and stability of the fiery energy of Leo is implicit. The background is tinged with the violet of Jupiter in Atziluth, whose watery nature works to balance out the dominant fire in this card.

Nine steady flames issue from the junctions of the wands, the number of Yesod and the Moon. The flames represent the feminine energy that balances out the fiery masculine energy and therefore brings harmony to this card. The nine flames also connect this card with the Nine of Wands, the "Strength" that is associated with "Victory."

Interpretation

Success after effort. Victory or triumph after strife. Balanced energy. Gain.

Reversed

Insolence. Pride. Arrogance.

Six of Wands

Title
Victory

Qabalistic Attribution
Tiphareth in Atziluth

Astrological Attribution
Jupiter in Leo

Seven of Wands

Title
Valor

Qabalistic Attribution
Netzach in Atziluth

Astrological Attribution
Mars in Leo

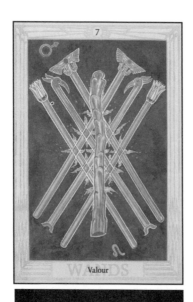

Description

An uneven wand or club dominates the Adept's wands from the previous card. The club is comprised of ten segments, suggesting a gross, material disruption of the balanced energy of the Six of Wands. The club is a weapon, and weapons are associated with Mars.

The heads of the Adepts' wands reflect the conflict between Mars and Venus (Netzach). The Lotus Wands are still blue because of their affinity with Venus, but the Phoenix Wands have tarnished to amber—the color of Netzach in Atziluth—and the Caduceus Wands are the red of Mars. The feet of the Phoenix Wands are also red, as if even here the martial energy has disrupted and overcome the weakness of Venus. The same idea holds for the club, which is amber giving way to red.

The flames at the junctions of the wands are wild and unsteady. Note that the astrological symbols are off center, reflecting the instability of the energy of this card. The background is deep purple, the color of Leo in Briah. The balanced Fire of Leo has, like the Adept's wands, been pushed to the background by the influence of Mars.

Interpretation

Opposition and conflict, yet courage to meet them. Bravery. A disordered and disorganized battle with an uncertain outcome, overcome only through individual effort.

Reversed

Fear. Cowardice. Retreat. Victory in small, insignificant things that consume energy needed for the true conflict. The querent is the underdog.

Description

Two overlapping pyramids form a star of eight points. This is the only card in the suit in which no flames appear; the wands have become eight red electrical rays. These rays emanate from the center, terminating in arrowheads that mark off the corners of the pyramids. The electric rays are symbols of Mercury, who rules both communication and technology. The rays also indicate the swiftness and speed attributed to this card, as electricity enables us to communicate at lightning speeds.

Above the pyramids is a rainbow, which is associated with Sagittarius and the Art card. The colors of the rainbow can also be seen in quicksilver, the metal of Mercury.

The pyramids, symbols of Chesed, reflect the various colors of the rainbow above them. The square-shaped pyramid is painted in colors corresponding to the saltire of Malkuth, while the diamond-shaped pyramid has no discernible color pattern. The apex of each pyramid is offset from the center to symbolize the difficulty that may arise in bringing the ethereal energies of this card into manifestation.

Interpretation

Rapidity. Speed. Haste. Approach to goal. Freedom. Communication.

Reversed

Too much force applied too quickly. A flash in the pan. Burnout. Impulsive violence. Impulsive behavior.

Eight of Wands

Title
Swiftness

Qabalistic Attribution
Hod in Atziluth

Astrological Attribution
Mercury in Sagittarius

Nine of Wands

Title
Strength

Qabalistic Attribution
Yesod in Atziluth

Astrological Attribution
Moon in Sagittarius

Description

Eight crossed arrows (wands) are dominated by a large wand crowned with the Sun and terminating in the Moon. The arrows are symbols of Sagittarius, and the wand resembles the path of Samekh (Sagittarius) that connects Tiphareth (Sun) and Yesod (Moon) on the Tree of Life. Six flames appear within the junction of the wands, a reference not only to the Sun but also to the Six of Wands.

The shafts of the arrows are the red of Fire. The feathers and head of the each arrow are silvery lunar crescents, nine in number. The Sun appears at the top of the card; it emits nine curved and nine straight rays, showing the influence of the Moon. The background is indigo, the color of Yesod in Atziluth.

The strength embodied within this card comes from the alignment and connection of the Sun, or conscious mind, with the Moon, the unconscious. This is accomplished through the path of Samekh, the directed will symbolized by the arrow of Sagittarius.[68]

As with the previous two cards, the Nine of Wands breaks with convention: both astrological sigils are placed at the bottom of the card, not above and below. The sigil of Sagittarius lies within the sphere of the Moon itself, symbolic of the seed (the Yod) of the directed will germinating in the unconscious.

Finally, the combination of the symbols of the Moon, Sagittarius, and the arrows evoke the image of huntress and lunar goddess Artemis. Her attri-

---

68.   Compare this card with the Art card.

butes of strength, determination, and independence are all in concordance with the energies of this card.

Interpretation

Power, force, or great strength intensified with direction.

Reversed

Rage. Raw, uncontrollable force directed in an impulsive and often negative manner. Wasted energy or force. Weakness.

Ten of Wands

Title
Oppression

Qabalistic Attribution
Malkuth in Atziluth

Astrological Attribution
Saturn in Sagittarius

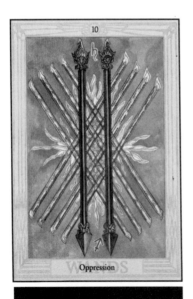

Description

Eight wands tipped with claws are crossed, and flames shoot from their junctions. The Dorjes from the Two of Wands have been stretched into bars that form a barrier to the wands and the fiery energy behind them. The power of the two Dorjes in the Two of Wands brought the unbridled energy of Chokmah under control. But the element of control so necessary at the top of the Tree becomes overbearing, oppressive, and restrictive in Malkuth. The claws and barbs on the crossed wands emphasize the severity of the force involved.

The optimism of Sagittarius has been crushed by the stern authoritarianism of Saturn. The Dorjes are black, a color associated with Saturn and Malkuth. The astrological sigils are totally confined by the Dorjes, and this is the only ten of the four suits where the suit symbols are not arranged according to the Tree of Life. This card is symbolically cut off from the rest of the Tree.

The background is orange, Geburah in Atziluth, which is the color associated with the Five of Wands. The influence of Geburah adds to the severity and conflict symbolized in this card.

Interpretation

Cruelty and malice. Revenge. Oppression. Repression. Fire in its most destructive aspect.

Reversed

Self-sacrifice or generosity in a destructive, oppressive situation.

Description

A single cup emerges from a large white lotus. A ray of light (the white brilliance of Kether in Briah) descends from the heavens and illuminates the water within the cup. Prismatic reflections and refractions emanate from their interplay.

On the front of the cup are three interlocking rings. This symbol also appears in the Hierophant, where it symbolizes the three Aeons of *The Book of the Law*. In the Old Aeon, the Ace of Cups portrayed the Holy Grail; in the Aeon of Horus it is the Cup of Babalon, the womb of all life.

The design in the background above the horizon suggests a seashell, symbolic of life beneath the water. Below the horizon is the Great Sea of Binah, the Primal Hé on the Tree who is known by the title Aima, the Bright Fertile Mother.

Interpretation

Fertility. Productiveness. Beauty. Pleasure. Happiness.

Reversed

Suggests that the means of attaining the well-dignified interpretations are blocked in a way that may be defined by the surrounding cards.

Ace of Cups

Title
The Root of the Powers of Water

Qabalistic Attribution
Kether in Briah

Tetragrammaton Attribution
Primal Hé

Ace of Cups

Two of Cups

Title

Love

Qabalistic Attribution

Chokmah in Briah

Astrological Attribution

Venus in Cancer

Description

A lotus floats on a green sea, and two dolphins are entwined around its stem. Water flows from the lotus at the top of the card in two streams, off the heads of the dolphins, and into two large cups in the foreground. Ten streams of water flow from the two cups into the water below.

The dolphin is traditionally attributed to Venus. In Greek mythology, the dolphin was originally sacred to Apollo and to Neptune. Crowley connects the dolphin to alchemy,[69] but there is no mention of the dolphin in any of the major alchemical texts, nor is it discussed in modern interpretations of alchemical symbolism. However, the dolphin does appear in one alchemical image, one that Crowley was probably familiar with. That image is the Great Hermetic Arcanum, a diagram taken from the seventeenth-century alchemical text *Musaeum Hermeticum*. It is shown and briefly described to the candidate in the Ritual of the Portal of the Golden Dawn.

In the Arcanum, the symbols of the masculine and the feminine are polarized. At the right, there is a queen crowned with a lunar crescent, riding a dolphin upon the waters. Balancing her on the left side of the image is a king with a solar nimbus sitting upon a lion, which is resting upon a hill. A salamander breathes fire below the lion.

As the counterpart to the lion, the dolphin is a symbol of the lunar/feminine principle, expand-

---

69. Crowley, *The Book of Thoth*, 196.

ing its scope from a single archetype among seven (or ten) planets to half of the lunar/solar duality. The polar nature of the dolphins, cups, and lotuses reflects the influence of Chokmah, the masculine force that balances out the many feminine elements of this card. Without Chokmah, this card would be much more unstable and unbalanced (see the Four of Cups).

The two dolphins both have red or rose bodies and yellow-gold fins, all solar colors. They are differentiated in two subtle ways. The most obvious difference is that the dolphin on the left has a yellow eye (Sun) and the dolphin on the right has a silver eye (Moon). A second, more obscure differentiation is found in the pectoral fins facing inward toward the lower stem. The fin of the solar (left) dolphin comes to five points, and the fifth trump is the Emperor, alchemical Sulfur. The fin of the lunar (right) dolphin comes to four points, and the fourth trump is the Empress, alchemical Salt.

The solar and lunar dolphins entwined symbolize the union of the masculine and feminine principles. The solar coloration of lunar symbols symbolizes the synthesis of the male and female principles; alchemically, each of the dolphins is a hermaphrodite, a symbol of alchemical Mercury. Remember that the fish is sacred not only to Venus but also to Mercury. Also note that through the influence of the dolphins, the lotus nourishes itself.

Instead of putting the astrological sigils of Venus and Cancer above and below the suit emblems as is traditional, Crowley has put them side by side, exalted above the horizon. This is appropriate, for the desirous, sensual sphere of Venus is very well placed in the sensitive and nurturing Cancer. The sigils are drawn in maroon, Cancer in Briah.

Ten streams of water fall from the cups, indicating that the qualities of this card will come to full manifestation. They fall into a sea painted in the colors of Venus.

Interpretation

Love under will. Harmony of masculine and feminine. Warm friendship. Pleasure in company. Harmony. Mirth. Marriage.

Reversed

The harsher aspects of love. Disharmonious union. Folly. Love at first sight. Obsession. Literally, "will under love."

Description

The cups are adorned with pomegranates, a reference to the myth of Persephone and Demeter. Persephone ate a pomegranate seed in the realm of Hades, which allowed him to hold her in the Underworld for four months each year as his bride. When Persephone returns to the land of the living, her mother Demeter rejoices and spring arrives; thus this card is representative of the warmth and fertility of the springtime.

The eight lotuses in this card refer to Mercury, the planetary attribution of this card. It was Mercury who relayed the message from Zeus begging for Persephone's release from the land of the dead, and it was he who carried her back to the land of the living in his chariot (Cancer). Eight is also the number of months that Persephone resided in the land of the living.

The yellow color of the lotuses suggests the influence of the Sun; the red color of the cups refers not only to the pomegranate but also to Aries, the sign that ushers in spring.

The cups overflow into the Great Sea of Binah. Demeter, the Greek goddess of agriculture and the harvest, is attributed to Binah. In fact, Demeter is a prime illustration of the two aspects of Binah. In the spring, Demeter resembles the Bright Fertile Mother as the plants of the earth sprout, grow, and flourish. In the winter, when vegetation withers and dies, she resembles the Dark Sterile Mother. Cancer, the most maternal sign of the zodiac, is well placed at the bottom of the card in the Sea of Binah.

Three of Cups

Title
Abundance

Qabalistic Attribution
Binah in Briah

Astrological Attribution
Mercury in Cancer

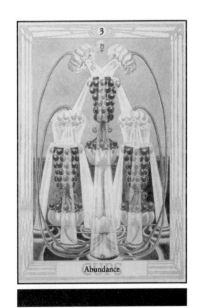

The seven streams that fall from the cups symbolize the love (seven is the number of Venus) that unites Persephone (Cups) and Demeter (Sea) and brings forth the spring.

Interpretation
Plenty. Pleasure. Hospitality. Sensuality. Joy. Fortune. Passive success. Fertility. Love, but not as balanced as in the Two of Cups.

Reversed
Waste. Transient pleasure. Extravagance in its negative aspects. The darker side of the myth of Persephone may manifest itself, and what was once plentiful and alive may become barren and die.

Description

The cups are arranged in a square. Water from the lotus fills the upper row of cups; they overflow into the lower cups, from which no water spills.

The weakness in this card is that all of its main attributions are associated with Water: Chesed (especially as Jupiter-Poseidon), Briah as the Primal Hé of the Tetragrammaton, the Moon, and Cancer. That the Moon is the ruler of Cancer only strengthens this watery imbalance.

At the same time, there is a distinct solar influence in this card. The lotus petals are pink, Tiphareth in Atziluth, and at the center of the lotus is a yellow disk. The four cups are yellow-gold, Tiphareth in Briah. Yet the cloudy sky and the lunar sigil that crowns the lotus suggest that this solar influence is not direct but reflected, just as sunlight is reflected off the surface of the Moon.

The cups have square bases, indicating the stability of Chesed. Yet while the upper cups rest firmly on the pads, the lower cups lack a stable base, suggesting the beginning of instability.

In the background, the sky is gray and foreboding, and the sea is slightly agitated, suggesting a storm is on the horizon. Hidden among the stems at the bottom of the card is a lemniscate, here symbolizing the infinite nature and unlimited potential of the Great Sea that is present in all of the cards of this suit.

Interpretation

Weakness. Abandonment to desire. Hedonism. Pleasure mixed with anxiety. Pleasure coming to an

Four of Cups

Title
Luxury

Qabalistic Attribution
Chesed in Briah

Astrological Attribution
Moon in Cancer

end. Temporary pleasure as an escape from a problem or situation (such as drug or alcohol use).

Reversed

Boredom. Weariness. Apathy. Burning out. Longing for something better.

Description

The cups are arranged in the shape of an inverted pentagram. Two lotuses in the center of the card are withering and bear forth no water.

The Fire of Geburah and Mars has overpowered the Watery elements of this card. The stems of the lotuses are red, and the lotuses are dry and drooping. The sky behind them glows a fiery orange. The cups are blue, the color of Water, but the water within them has evaporated.

The cups in this card resemble the Cup of Stolistes, which has a square base, a spherical stem, and a crescent-shaped bowl (see figure 6). The Cup of Stolistes is used in the purification of the temple and officers in Golden Dawn rituals. The fact that the cups are empty defeats their purpose; there is no water to be used in purification, and the water below is corrupted through putrefaction. The inverted pentagram, which signifies Spirit dominated by the four elements, conveys the same idea.

Figure 6: The Cup of Stolistes

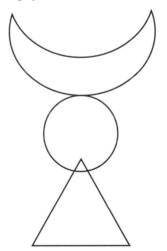

Title
Disappointment

Qabalistic Attribution
Geburah in Briah

Astrological Attribution
Mars in Scorpio

Disappointment

129

Mars is the ruler of Scorpio, the only harmonious relationship between Fire and Water found in this card. The greenish-gray waters suggest the putrefaction of Scorpio, while the reddish waves indicate Mars as the heat associated with putrefaction. This harmony is also signified in the sigil of Mars, which is drawn in blue and orange, the flashing colors of elemental Water.

Interpretation

Disappointment. End of pleasure. Misfortune. Disturbance when least expected. Loss or end of friendship or relationship. Sadness. Trouble from unexpected or unsuspected sources. Possibly deceit, treachery, or ill will.

Reversed

Emotional stability. Coping skills. Determination and fortitude to overcome misfortune and anxiety.

Description

The cups are arranged in a hexagram with the Sun in the center, an arrangement based on the Tree of Life. The lotuses are yellow, the color of Tiphareth in Briah, and the cups are also painted in solar colors. Water does not overflow from the cups but appears to swirl about within them.

The bases of the cups are composed of five spheres (the fifth is hidden but required for balance), suggesting Mars; also forming the base of the cup is the sigil of Aries. Mars in Aries is the attribution of the Two of Wands, titled Dominion, suggesting that the pleasure symbolized in the Six of Cups ultimately results from the establishment and direction of the energy of the Two of Wands.

The putrefying sea of the Five of Cups has become blue and fertile. The Sun brings out the more positive qualities of Scorpio: passion, desire, and pleasure. The ten lotus stems evident at the bottom of the card suggest that the pleasure has material origins, evoking the intense carnality associated with Scorpio.

Interpretation

Beginning of pleasure. The pleasure indicated by this card is due to the harmony of natural forces and not necessarily the fulfillment of desire. Optimism. Fulfillment of sexual will.

Reversed

Pleasure disturbed, usually through the actions of the querent, but the true nature of this disruption is defined by the surrounding cards. Pleasure gained at the expense of others.

Six of Cups

Title
Pleasure

Qabalistic Attribution
Tiphareth in Briah

Astrological Attribution
Sun in Scorpio

Seven of Cups

Title

Debauch

Qabalistic Attribution

Netzach in Briah

Astrological Attribution

Venus in Scorpio

Description

The cups are arranged in two descending triangles over a larger cup. This arrangement suggests the Tree of Life below the Abyss, cut off from the influence of Binah, and therefore the Great Sea at the bottom of the card is poisoned and corrupted. The lotuses appear to be diseased, and the slime they exude is emerald, the color of Netzach in Briah.

The sigil of Venus is blue, the color of water. The sigil of Scorpio is vivid indigo brown, Scorpio in Assiah, indicating the lowest qualities of Scorpio. Venus is in its detriment in Scorpio, suggesting that the planet's emotional nature is not expressed; instead it is putrefied and hidden, in affinity with the darker side of Scorpio. The darkening sky and approaching storm signify the ominous buildup of emotion and energy that accompanies this repression.

Finally, note that the ripples in the poisonous sea are violet, the color of Yesod (Luna) in Briah, and that Luna is in her fall in Scorpio. The corrupting and putrefying elements of Scorpio are the true poison of this card.

Interpretation

Corruption of pleasure. Delusion. Illusory success. Lying. Deceit. Deception. Drunkenness or drug abuse. Promises unfulfilled. May also denote lust, cheap sex, or violence within an emotional relationship.

Reversed

Relaxation. Loosening up and letting go. Respite. Vacation. Time out to decompress and recharge.

Description

The cups are cracked and broken and have small, unstable bases. The top row of cups is empty. Water from two diseased lotuses fills the two middle cups; they overflow into two cups at the bottom, but the center bottom cup remains empty. The two lowest cups are not even half full.

The cups stand on pools of stagnant water scattered on infertile ground. Above them are dark clouds of indigo, the color of Saturn in Atziluth. Saturn weighs down Pisces, which is already prone to inertia. Furthermore, Mercury (Hod) is in its detriment in Pisces, which suppresses the energy and speed of Mercury in this card. The only hope of escape is symbolized by the yellowish light on the horizon, representative of the energy of Tiphareth that is needed to overcome the inertia of Saturn.

Interpretation

Abandoned success through indolence (laziness). Disease. Misery. Decline of interest in anything. Wandering from place to place. Depression. Emotional dissatisfaction. Lack of creativity. Emptiness. Discontent. Stagnation of thought or emotion. Suicide. Abandonment. Infertility.

Reversed

Motivation. Self-preservation. Creative impulse. Cautious optimism. Potential to improve.

Eight of Cups

Title
Indolence

Qabalistic Attribution
Hod in Briah

Astrological Attribution
Saturn in Pisces

Indolence

Nine of Cups

Title
Happiness

Qabalistic Attribution
Yesod in Briah

Astrological Attribution
Jupiter in Pisces

Description

The cups overflow with water from nine lotuses. The cups are violet, the color of Yesod and Jupiter in Briah. They are arranged in a square, a figure attributed to Jupiter and associated with stability and manifestation.

Jupiter is the ruler of Pisces, allowing for expansion and growth. The sky is blue, the color of Jupiter in Briah, indicating the expansive nature of the planet. The cups rest upon the placid waters of Pisces. Yesod bears forth the influence of the Moon, which emphasizes the creative and pleasurable aspects of Water.

The sigils of Jupiter and Pisces are drawn in the colors of Atziluth, violet and crimson.

Interpretation

Pleasure and happiness, complete and fully realized or experienced. Sensuality.

Reversed

Overindulgence. Unrealized happiness. Self-denial of happiness or pleasure.

Description

The cups are arranged in the form of the Tree of Life. The intricate stem of the lotus in the background forms the paths between the Sephirotic cups, with the three Supernals located within the flower. The cup in Kether, filled by the topmost petal of the lotus, distributes water to all of the cups below it. The cups of the middle pillar overflow.

The sigil of Mars is placed on the cup in Kether, bringing out the planet's highest and most spiritual qualities. The streams of water that flow from the body of the cup in Kether and across the Abyss are five in number, an allusion to the transmission and manifestation of the spiritualized forces of Mars. The sigil of Pisces on the bottom cup is drenched in water, its native element, and Malkuth brings further stability to the energies of this card.

The background is painted in Martial colors. The rose is drawn in bright scarlet (Geburah in Yetzirah), the stem in scarlet (Geburah in Briah), and the sky is orange (Geburah in Atziluth). Only the color of Geburah in Assiah, the red of Mars flecked with the black of Earth, is absent in this card. This arrangement indicates that the lowest and material qualities of Mars are not expressed.

Finally, consider that the fiery force of Mars can be used not only to energize the placidity and stagnation of Pisces but also to provide the momentum needed to move the wheel of the zodiac from Pisces into Aries, who is ruled by Mars and represents the onset of spring. The cups resemble the sigil of Aries as if to indicate this transition.

Ten of Cups

Title
Satiety

Qabalistic Attribution
Malkuth in Briah

Astrological Attribution
Mars in Pisces

Interpretation

Complete and lasting success. Matters arranged and settled as wished. Peacemaking.

Reversed

Disruption of success, sometimes violent. Waste. Exhaustion. Rivalry. Attack from below.

Description

The sword that dominates this card is the Great Sword of the Magician. The hilt is made of copper (Venus), and the blade is made of steel (Mars). The sword is green, the mixture of yellow (Sun) and blue (Water). The hilt of the sword is placed squarely in the Sun of Tiphareth; the sphere of the pommel is the center point of the solar sphere behind it. A serpent is coiled six times around the hilt of the sword, also identifying it with Tiphareth and Vau. The guard is formed by two crescent moons that balance out the solar energy.

The blade is inscribed with the word *Thelema*, or Will. The suit of Swords represents the intellect or Ruach, but the Great Sword of the Magician is symbolic of the True Will. It pierces the crown of Kether, which is white on the outside and yellow on the inside to indicate the harmonious relationship between God (Kether) and the Adept (Tiphareth).

In the background, the Sun rises over the water, a reference to Air manifesting as the union of Fire and Water. The power of the sword has burned away the clouds and brought clarity and light to the intellect. At the top of the card, one can see the stars in the night sky, the body of Nuit.

Interpretation

Invoked force (as opposed to the natural force of the Ace of Wands). Represents great power for good or evil brought into existence by the will or intellect.

Reversed

Suggests that the means of realizing the well-dignified interpretations are blocked in a way that may be defined by the surrounding cards.

Ace of Swords

Title
The Root of
the Powers of Air

Qabalistic Attribution
Kether in Yetzirah

**Tetragrammaton
Attribution**
Vau

Two of Swords

Title
Peace

Qabalistic Attribution
Chokmah in Yetzirah

Astrological Attribution
Moon in Libra

Description

The two swords are crossed and united in a blue rose. At the top of the card the symbol of the Moon is balanced upon a dagger, and at the bottom of the card another dagger supports the sigil of Libra. The Moon suggests calm and peace, and Libra brings further balance to the card. The guard of each sword is comprised of symbols of peace: angelic figures kneeling in prayer and a dove.

The rose is the blue pearl-gray of Chokmah in Yetzirah. The Qabalistic Part of the Soul that corresponds to Chokmah is the Chiah, the True Will, the force behind all forces that maintains the balance in this card.[70]

The background is bright yellow-green, the color of Netzach in Yetzirah. The geometric patterns that appear in the background of the suit of Swords are swastikas, which represent the constant activity of Air.

Interpretation

Peace. Peace restored. Balance of emotional and intellectual aspects of a situation. Harmony.

Reversed

Inactivity. Indecision. End of peace. Disruption of balance, especially between intellectual and emotional forces.

---

70.   See the Two of Wands.

Description

The rose from the previous card has been torn apart by the swords. The bottom sword is modeled after the Great Sword of the Magician from the Ace of Swords, but the guard is much shorter, the blade much more pointed, and it lacks the inscription of Thelema. This inferior version of the Great Sword holds the rose in place, while the upper two swords pick it apart. The swords are tinted with the green of Libra.

Saturn is exalted in Libra, but the influence of Binah overwhelms this card with Saturnine energy, weighing it down, bearing forth limitation and restriction. Binah is here Aima, the Dark Sterile Mother, symbolized by the black, stormy sea in the background of the card.

This card is indeed a glyph of the Trance of Sorrow, which must be realized in order to travel the road to the Neschamah in Binah. In this card it is all too evident that the intuition and intelligence of the Neschamah has not yet been realized.

Interpretation

Sorrow. Disruption. Separation. Melancholy. Unhappiness. Tears.

Reversed

Faithfulness. Honesty. Singing.

Three of Swords

Title
Sorrow

Qabalistic Attribution
Binah in Yetzirah

Astrological Attribution
Saturn in Libra

Four of Swords

Title
Truce

Qabalistic Attribution
Chesed in Yetzirah

Astrological Attribution
Jupiter in Libra

Description

The swords are symmetrically arranged over a green St. Andrew's cross, their points sheathed in a rose of forty-nine petals.[71] The guard on each sword has a design identifying it with one of the four elements: waves for Water, flames for Fire, a chaotic design that suggests the activity of Air, and disks for Earth.

The green cross resembles the Rose Cross. The cross is the green of Libra. The rose of forty-nine petals (seven by seven) represents social harmony. It is the mystic number of Venus, the ruler of Libra. The rose is also symbolic of spirit, which here unifies the four elements (the Swords), employing the forces of Chesed (Mercy) and Gedulah (Love).

The background is the blue of Jupiter and Chesed, accenting the yellow rays that spike forth in roughly symmetrical patterns. The yellow represents the Air attribution of the suit. The astrological symbols are drawn in deep purple, Chesed in Yetzirah.

Interpretation

Convention. Compromise. Rest from strife. Refuge from mental chaos. Recovery from sickness. Peace after war. Relaxation of anxiety. May be a temporary situation according to surrounding cards.

Reversed

Stalemate. Forced compromise. A temporary truce, rest, or peace; the conflict will soon resume.

---

71. The St. Andrew's cross is named for the Apostle who, believing himself to be unworthy of being crucified upon the same cross as Christ, asked to be executed upon a diagonal cross.

Description

The swords have completely shredded the rose of the previous cards, and its petals have turned from white to bright scarlet, the color of Geburah in Yetzirah. The petals have been arranged in the shape of an inverted pentagram, with the hilts of the swords arranged as the points of the star. The blades meet in the center of the pentagram.

The lowest hilt bears a crown, representative of Spirit. The inverted pentagram is symbolic of the domination of Spirit by the elements, and thus the blade of the Spirit-sword is broken. Each of the remaining hilts may be attributed to one of the four elements. The green serpent represents Earth, the fish is Water, the red hilt indicates Fire, and the final hilt is the number six, which is the number of Tiphareth and Vau, Air.

Venus is not well-placed in Aquarius, whose individualistic and dispassionate nature clashes with the planet of relationships. The swords of the intellect have shredded the rose, symbolic of love and emotion. Venus is overwhelmed by the fiery energy of Mars (Geburah), and so the sigil of Venus is drawn in the flashing colors of Fire, green (Venus) and red (Mars).

The background is tinted with the green of Venus and the colors of Aquarius in the Four Worlds: violet; sky blue; bluish mauve; and white, tinged purple.

Interpretation

Defeat. Weakness. Failure. Conflict decided against a person. Loss. In relationships, it may signify malice, spite, slander, or dishonor.

Reversed

Grief. Mourning. Recovery from defeat or failure. The aftermath of the situation.

Five of Swords

Title
Defeat

Qabalistic Attribution
Geburah in Yetzirah

Astrological Attribution
Venus in Aquarius

Six of Swords

Title
Science

Qabalistic Attribution
Tiphareth in Yetzirah

Astrological Attribution
Mercury in Aquarius

Description

The swords are arranged in a circle, their points meeting in a Rose Cross. The hilts of the swords are painted in the colors of the planetary paths in Atziluth: yellow for Mercury, violet for Jupiter, blue for the Moon, indigo for Saturn, scarlet for Mars, and emerald green for Venus. The planetary swords are brought into balance by the Sun, indicated by the golden cross of six squares. The Rose Cross is a symbol of the unification of the macrocosm and the microcosm, the completion of the Great Work.

Tiphareth is the seat of the Ruach, the conscious mind. This card shows the faculty of the Ruach fully realized, working in harmony with the other Qabalistic Parts of the Soul associated with the planetary Sephiroth. Mercury is exalted in Aquarius, strengthening the intellectual qualities of this card. The astrological sigils are violet, the color of Hod (Mercury) and Aquarius in Atziluth.

Lady Harris explains the curious pattern in the background of this card: "[The swords] are lying on a fencer's diagram (14th century) which was worked out scientifically to show the positions in which a fencer can stand and be invulnerable."[72]

Interpretation

Intelligence that has reached its goal. Mental labor or work. Success after anxiety or trouble. Patience. Possibly a journey by water or by air.

Reversed

Intellectual pride. Conceit. Intellectualization of nonscientific problems.

---

72. Wasserman, *Instructions for Aleister Crowley's Thoth Tarot Deck*, 47.

Description

Six swords are arranged in a crescent formation, pointing downward against a larger sword. The hilts of the swords are comprised of planetary symbols, with the larger sword bearing the symbol of the Sun.

The larger sword represents the Ruach in Tiphareth; it strains against the other parts of the mind, represented by the planetary symbols. Venus, Mars, Jupiter, and Mercury represent other elements of the Ruach; Saturn is the Neschamah, the link to the supernal elements; and the Moon, symbolized by the hilt with rings that form lunar crescents, is representative of the Nephesh. This futile struggle is driven by the emotions, the influence of Netzach and the Moon, which cloud and distort the intellectual qualities of Aquarius and Yetzirah. The Sun is in its fall in Aquarius, also weakening the Ruach.

The background is cold pale blue, the color of the Moon in Yetzirah, while the swords are white-tinged purple, the color of Aquarius in Assiah. Unlike the rest of the cards in this suit, the swastikas in the background of the Seven of Swords are arranged asymmetrically, symbolic of disorder and instability.

Interpretation

Unstable effort. Vacillation. Striving against opposition too powerful to overcome. Unreliability. An untrustworthy person. Giving up on the brink of winning due to lack of energy. Possibly also a journey by land.

Reversed

Support. Assistance. Unexpected help. Good advice.

Seven of Swords

Title
Futility

Qabalistic Attribution
Netzach in Yetzirah

Astrological Attribution
Moon in Aquarius

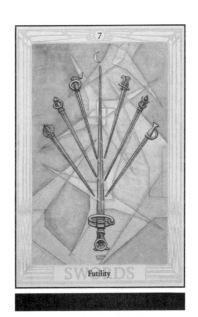

Eight of Swords

Title
Interference

Qabalistic Attribution
Hod in Yetzirah

Astrological Attribution
Jupiter in Gemini

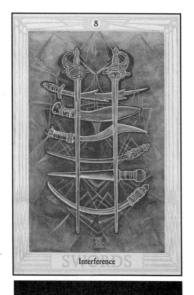

Description

Two long swords form a barrier to six shorter swords, illustrative of the titles of this card: "Interference" and "Shortened Force." The smaller blades named in *The Book of Thoth* (the kris, kukri, scramasax, dagger, machete, and yataghan) are not full swords; most can be described as knives.[73] This again alludes to the idea of shortened force.

Jupiter is in its fall in Gemini, the inquisitive nature of the sign hindering the planet of expansion. The astrological sigils and the swastikas behind the swords are drawn blue and orange, the flashing colors of elemental Water. This suggests that the cause of the interference is emotional in nature, as uncontrolled or intense emotions can form a barrier to rational thinking.

Interpretation

Restriction. Interference. Attention to details at the expense of more important things. Lack of persistence. Unforeseen bad luck. An obstacle in the querent's path. Emotion obstructing rational thinking.

Reversed

Obstacles, interference, and so forth, as mentioned above, but easier to overcome.

---

73. Crowley, *The Book of Thoth,* 207.

Description

Nine swords of varying lengths are arranged with their points downward, dripping blood. Drops of yellowish poison fall from above; the colors in the background become darker and more menacing as the poison and blood descend.

The jagged blades are the red of Mars. The rust that scars the blades is a degradation of iron, another attribution of Mars. The blood dripping from the blades emphasizes the ideas of pain and suffering. The cruel, aggressive energy of Mars in Gemini overwhelms the more passive and receptive energy of Yesod and the Moon. Yesod is the seat of the Nephesch, the animal soul of man, the primal emotions and desires inimical to reason.

The sigil of Mars is red, and the sigil of Gemini is painted in the flashing color of green. The drops of poison fall behind the swords, not from their blades. The poison ends where the blood begins to fall, suggesting that it is the poison, symbolic of malice or cruelty, that leads to the pain of bloodletting.

Interpretation

Despair. Cruelty. Suffering. Pain. Loss. Illness. Pain of oppression, burden, or shame.

Reversed

A painful lesson to be learned. Pain, despair, cruelty or suffering lessening or decreasing but not ending; the situation will not end but only improve, at least temporarily.

Nine of Swords

Title
Cruelty

Qabalistic Attribution
Yesod in Yetzirah

Astrological Attribution
Mars in Gemini

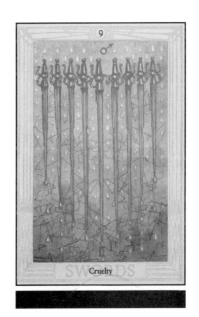

Ten of Swords

Title
Ruin

Qabalistic Attribution
Malkuth in Yetzirah

Astrological Attribution
Sun in Gemini

Description

The hilts of the ten swords are arranged in the pattern of the Sephiroth. Nine swords have destroyed the central sword in Tiphareth.

The five upper swords are responsible for shattering the sword of Tiphareth, and in studying their relationship an interesting pattern may be found. The hilts in Chesed and Geburah are Tau crosses, symbols of Saturn. The hilts in Chokmah and Binah are hourglasses, symbols of time and thus also of Saturn. The hilt of Kether is a set of scales, a symbol of Libra, which is exalted in Saturn. This implies that the most destructive elements of Saturn are at work here: limitation, depression, sterility, aging, and death.

The four lower swords hold the sword of Tiphareth in place. The hilts in Hod and Netzach, with their four-pronged guards, show the same Saturnine influence as the Tau crosses above them, with an emphasis on limitation and restriction. The hilt in Yesod has the sigil of the Sun at its center, and the hilt in Malkuth shows a pentagram (the symbol of man) and the crescent of Luna. Consciousness has been forced into the shadowy realm of the unconscious, and the unconscious impulses have come to the surface.

The ten white and yellow rays emanating from Tiphareth indicate a physical manifestation of the destruction that occurs in this card. The background is a fiery orange with red swastikas, colors of Mars. In ancient astrology, Mars was referred to as the "Lesser Malefic," and Saturn was known as the "Greater Malefic"; both lend their malignance to the energies of this card.

Interpretation

Reason divorced from reality. Failure. Disaster. Physical death. Spiritually, it may signal the end of delusion.

Reversed

A brush with death. Realization of mortality. Tragedy averted but not without significant cost.

Ace of Disks

Title
The Root of the Powers of Earth

Qabalistic Attribution
Kether in Assiah

Astrological Attribution
None

Description

The disk on this card bears the seal of *To Mega Therion*, Greek for "the Great Beast," Aleister Crowley's motto as Magus. Crowley identified himself with the Beast of Revelation and was also identified as the Beast in *The Book of the Law*.

At the center of the disk is the Mark of the Beast, which resembles the phallus and testicles. The circles are painted in the yellow of Tiphareth to emphasize the connection with the Sun. This solar energy is balanced by a white crescent in the center of the sigil representing the Moon. Inscribed in red within the testicles is the number 666, the number of the Beast in Revelation and the numeration of *Therion*, "beast" in Greek gematria. Six is the number of the Sun, and 666 is the sum of all numbers in the Magical Square of the Sun.

The Mark of the Beast is inscribed within the seven-pointed Star of Babalon. The phallus and testes are placed within the womb formed by the Star. Together they are a glyph of Babalon and the Beast conjoined, the masculine and feminine archetypes of Thelema united in the act of creation.

Surrounding this glyph is a decagram, which symbolizes Malkuth, the Kingdom of manifestation. The decagram forms the hub of a wheel of ten spokes, indicating the constant motion and activity of the suit symbol. The interior of this wheel is salmon, the color of Tiphareth in Yetzirah, and the rim of the wheel is the yellow-gold of Tiphareth in Briah. The motto *To Mega Therion* is inscribed on the wheel in the golden amber of Tiphareth in Assiah.

Behind the disk are two translucent brown ovals that signify the unification of the lingam and the yoni. This figure is borne upon four pair of wings, which in turn are sheltered by two sets of wings in the background, painted in the green of Earth flecked with the yellow of the Sun. The wings indicate the blessing of Kether and the spiritualization of the element of Earth.

Interpretation

Spirit manifest as pure materialism in all senses. Physical creation and conception. The connection between the spiritual and material worlds. This card is greatly affected by dignity, usually expressed as loss or gain.

Reversed

Suggests that the means of attaining the well-dignified interpretations are blocked in a way that may be defined by the surrounding cards.

Two of Disks

Title

Change

Qabalistic Attribution

Chokmah in Assiah

Astrological Attribution

Jupiter in Capricorn

Description

The disks are yin-yang symbols set on white and black disks and encircled by a crowned serpent.

The "eyes" of the yin-yang symbols are inscribed with the sigils of the four elements and are painted in the appropriate elemental colors. The upper sections of the two disks are painted in green gray and plum, Virgo in Yetzirah and Assiah. Virgo is Yod, the letter attributed to Chokmah when the Tetragrammaton is projected onto the Tree of Life. The lower half of each disk is yellow, the color of Mercury in Atziluth.

The coils of the serpent house opposing forces: yin and yang; the active and passive elements; the white and black disks; the spiritual devotion of Jupiter and the gross materialism of Capricorn. The serpent embodies the constant movement between the two poles, the change that is stability.

The serpent is a symbol of wisdom, the meaning of Chokmah. It wears a yellow crown, the color of Mercury in Atziluth. The Mercurial crown has seven points, identifying it with Venus (Netzach) and declaring its nature to be Love in contrast with the serpent itself, which is Will. To that end, the serpent is adorned with octagonal spots or scales, eight being the number of Mercury (Hod). Mercury is associated with Chokmah as the Logos, and the Logos of the Aeon of Horus is Thelema, or Will.

The sigil of Capricorn is drawn in green gray, while the sigil of Jupiter is plum, colors of Virgo in Yetzirah and Assiah. The background is violet and indigo, Jupiter and Capricorn in Atziluth.

Interpretation

Harmonious change. Alternation (gain and loss, weakness and strength, elation and melancholy, and so on). Journeying or wandering.

Reversed

Disharmonious change. Change that brings a negative result. Inconsistency. Lack of focus in effort.

Three of Disks

Title
Work

Qabalistic Attribution
Binah in Assiah

Astrological Attribution
Mars in Capricorn

Description

The disks are wheels that form the base of a pyramid. The wheels are the red of Mars to show energy and action. Mars is exalted in Capricorn, contributing constructive energy to the card. The wheels are marked with the alchemical symbols for Mercury, Sulfur, and Salt. The three alchemical principles are equally balanced, working in harmony to project the pyramid.

The color of the pyramid approaches white-flecked red, blue, and yellow—the colors of Chokmah in Assiah, where force begins to take form. The pyramid is only a projection, for a true solid can only manifest below the Abyss.

The Great Sea of Binah has solidified due to the influence of Capricorn, which marks the Winter Solstice. However, the ice has melted around the wheels and the pyramid, indicative of the fiery energy of Mars. The background is indigo, the color of Capricorn in Atziluth, and green, the color of the element of Earth.

Interpretation

Commerce. Construction. Material creation. Paid employment.

Reversed

Mismanagement. Delay in business matters, sometimes resulting in loss. Sometimes selfishness or greed. May indicate seeking the impossible.

Description

The disks are the towers of a fortress, each marked with a symbol of the four elements. The fortress has four walls and gates at the north, east, and west with the main gate at the south. There are six crenellations on each wall, the number of the Sun. A deep blue moat with a yellow wave pattern surrounds the fortress, and the pattern of the land beyond suggests that the fortress sits upon a hill.

Material power is the only thing to be gained in this card. Only the southern gate into the fortress is open, the path leading to Malkuth, an idea reinforced by the symbol of Capricorn (an Earth sign) on the path. The northern path, inscribed with the Sun, is inaccessible from the fortress of the four Elements. The indirect influence of the Sun in this card is indicated by the solar colors in the background.

The moat is deep azure, flecked yellow, the color of Chesed in Assiah. Stability, order, and law are all characteristics of this Sephira.

The Two of Disks also contains the symbols of the four elements. In the Two of Disks they are in a constant state of movement and change, while in the Four they are separated, structured, and stable.

Interpretation

Earthly power but nothing beyond. Security. Law and order. Skill in the direction and management of physical forces.

Reversed

Prejudice. Covetousness. Suspicion. Lack of originality.

Four of Disks

Title
Power

Qabalistic Attribution
Chesed in Assiah

Astrological Attribution
Sun in Capricorn

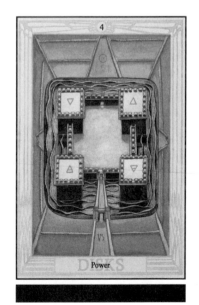

Five of Disks

Title
Worry

Qabalistic Attribution
Geburah in Assiah

Astrological Attribution
Mercury in Taurus

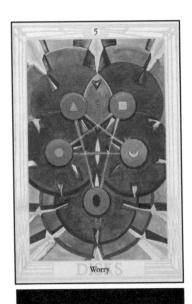

Description

The five disks are arranged in an inverted pentagram, following the pattern established in the Five of Cups and the Five of Swords. Hindu tattwas have been assigned to the disks; the black egg of Spirit is at the lowest point of the pentagram, symbolizing the triumph of matter over Spirit. The disks obscure the light in the background, another allusion to the triumph of matter over Spirit.

The disks are bent and torn by strain. They resemble gears, locked and immobile; the machinery is jammed and the labor is suspended. The speed and fluidity of Mercury has collided with the slowness and solidity of Taurus, adding to the strain present in this card. The force of Geburah is also weighed down by the earthy nature of Taurus and Assiah.

The astrological sigils are drawn in the flashing colors of Water. The dark bluish grays of the disks are accented with yellow and violet, the flashing colors of Air. There is no red or green to represent Fire in this card, and even the red triangle of Tejas has faded into violet. Thus while Water, Air, and Earth are noticeably represented, there is no Fire to provide the energy to break out of the strain and inertia symbolized in this card.

Interpretation

Intense strain with continued inaction, especially in spiritual matters. Loss of money or profession. Monetary anxiety.

Reversed

Labor. Land cultivation. Building. Intelligence applied to labor.

Description

The disks are arranged in a hexagram, with the planets arranged in the form of the Tree of Life. In the center of the hexagram is a blue-lined rose of forty-nine petals placed over a red cross of five squares. The Rose Cross is surrounded by circles and hexagrams painted in the colors of Tiphareth: clear pink rose, yellow-gold, rich salmon, and gold amber.

The Rose Cross represents the integration of the energies of Geburah (red cross) and Chesed (blue rose) within the sphere of Tiphareth. This symbol is identical to the Rose and Cross at the Head of the Pastos found in the Adeptus Minor Ritual of the Golden Dawn (see figure 7).[74] Following this and other examples, the diagonal rays behind this symbol would be inscribed with the letters INRI, the formula of Tiphareth and the Sun.

Figure 7: The Rose and Cross at the Head of the Pastos

74. Regardie, *The Golden Dawn*, 243.

Six of Disks

Title

Success

Qabalistic Attribution

Tiphareth in Assiah

Astrological Attribution

Moon in Taurus

The Moon is exalted in Taurus, a relationship that brings fecundity and manifestation to this card. The disks are blue, the color of the Moon in Atziluth, and the sigils of the planets are drawn in red-orange, Taurus in Atziluth. The background is composed of the blue tones of the Moon and the browns of Taurus. The six green-lined rays that spring from the intersections of the disks signify the balanced, fertile energies at work in this card.

Interpretation

Success and gain in material things. Material power, rank, influence, or nobility. Possibly philanthropy.

Reversed

Prodigality. Conceit with wealth. Financial management problems. Insolence.

Description

The disks are arranged in the geomantic figure Rubeus, considered to be the most malignant of the sixteen figures of geomancy. In geomantic divination, Rubeus gives a bad result for the querent in almost every instance. Furthermore, the Golden Dawn attributes Mars in Scorpio to this geomantic figure;[75] Mars and Venus (Netzach) are opposites, and Venus is in its detriment in Scorpio.

This card bears the most unfavorable aspects of Earth. The disks are stamped with images of Saturn and Taurus. The slow and restrictive nature of Saturn combined with the slow-moving and material traits of Taurus bring inertia and stagnation to this card. Life depends on change; thus, the vegetation in the background is dying. Saturn (Binah) represents the influence of Ama, the Dark Sterile Mother that has here defeated the fecundity of Venus (Netzach).

Colorwise, this card is the darkest card in the deck. The disks are surrounded with faded bands of red and blue, masculine and feminine energy stifled by bands of olive and brown, the colors of Taurus in Yetzirah and Assiah.

Interpretation

Little gain for much labor. Labor abandoned. Promises of success unfulfilled. Hopes deceived or crushed. Disappointment. Slavery. Necessity. Unprofitable speculation.

Reversed

Delay but growth. Charity. A labor with no expectation of material gain.

---

75. Regardie, *The Golden Dawn*, 526–527.

Seven of Disks

Title
Failure

Qabalistic Attribution
Netzach in Assiah

Astrological Attribution
Saturn in Taurus

Eight of Disks

Title
Prudence

Qabalistic Attribution
Hod in Assiah

Astrological Attribution
Sun in Virgo

Description

The disks are flowers and fruits of a tree growing in fertile land. The fruits are the orange of Hod in Briah, with a green dot in the middle to indicate the fertility of Venus (Netzach). The flowers are the plum color of Virgo in Assiah. Virgo represents Earth in its most feminine form, and the sign is identified with the virtue of prudence in connection with the Hermit. Mercury is the ruler of Virgo, a planet that is also associated with the Hermit in the Lovers.

Each fruit is divided into five segments, and each flower has five petals. Five is the number of the Hebrew letter Hé, the Mother of the Tetragrammaton, associated with nature and fertility. Taken as a whole, the segments and petals add up to ten, the number of Malkuth and manifestation.

The disks are attached to the tree with orange stalks and are sheltered by large green leaves, reflecting the balance of Hod and Netzach found in the fruits. The trunk of the tree is slate gray, the color of Virgo in Briah. The fertile soil in the background is given the colors of Venus and Virgo. Behind the tree, the sky is yellow fading into orange, showing the influences of Mercury and the Sun.

The sigil of Virgo is drawn in the orange of Hod, while the sigil of the Sun is drawn in plum with a green dot in the center, identifying it with the fruits of the tree and indicating the vital role of the Sun in agriculture.

Interpretation

Prudence. Caution. Building. Carefulness. Intelligence applied to material affairs. Agriculture. Slow, steady gain. Possibly cunning.

Reversed

Too much attention paid to small details. Avarice. Hoarding. Worry. "Penny wise and pound foolish" attitudes.

Nine of Disks

Title
Gain

Qabalistic Attribution
Yesod in Assiah

Astrological Attribution
Venus in Virgo

Description

Three central disks of rose, green, and blue form an upright triangle. They are placed between six coins arranged in a hexagram, with each disk inscribed with a profile derived from its planetary sigil.

The central disks represent the influence of the three most fertile planets: rose for the Sun; green for Venus, and blue for the Moon. Rays of the three colors intermingled emanate from the junction of these disks, projecting fertility and abundance. The planetary disks also benefit from this energy, surrounded by bands of blue, green, and rose. Venus is in its fall in Virgo, but this detrimental relationship is not reflected in the symbolism of this card, nor does it affect the overall meaning.

The astrological sigils are drawn in the plum of Virgo in Assiah. The background is a patchwork of yellowish green, slate gray, green gray, and plum, the colors of Virgo in the Four Worlds. It resembles cultivated fields ready for harvest.

Interpretation

Good luck attending material affairs. Inheritance. Favor. Gain. Increase of wealth.

Reversed

Gain at the expense of others. Covetousness. Theft. Disfavor.

Description

The disks are arranged in the pattern of the Sephiroth, and each bears a symbol of Mercury as follows:

1. *Kether.* The astrological sigil of Mercury.

2. *Chokmah.* The sigils of the planets unified in that of Mercury.

3. *Binah.* The symbol of Mercury as drawn on the Tree of Life. (Note the spheres in the sigil.)

4. *Chesed.* The Enochian letter *Pe*, which corresponds to the letter *B* in English and thus the Hebrew letter *Beth*, which is the Magus and Mercury.

5. *Geburah.* The Hebrew letter *Beth*, associated with the Magus and Mercury.

6. *Tiphareth.* Hebrew for "Raphael," the Archangel of Tiphareth and the Angel of Mercury.

7. *Netzach.* An eight-pointed star; eight is the number of Hod and Mercury.

8. *Hod.* A hexagram inscribed within a hexagon, both solar figures. The combined energy of the Sun and Mercury (Hod) is necessary to overcome the inertia inherent in the element of Earth. The hexagram inscribed in a hexagon also relates to Mercury: 6 x 6 = 36 = the mystic number of Mercury (1 + 2 + 3 + 4 + 5 + 6 + 7 + 8 = 36).

Title
Wealth

Qabalistic Attribution
Malkuth in Assiah

Astrological Attribution
Mercury in Virgo

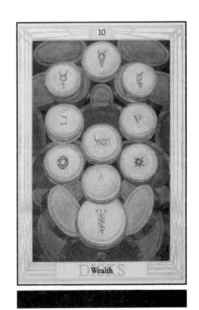

9. *Yesod.* A pyramid composed of the mystic numbers of Mercury.[76]

    8 is the number of Hod and Mercury.

    64 is the number of squares in the magick square, or Kamea of Mercury.

    260 is the sum of the numbers in any row, column, or diagonal line of the magick square. It is also the gematria of Tiriel, the Intelligence of Mercury.

    2080 is the sum of all of the numbers in the magick square. It is also the gematria of Taphtharharath, the Spirit of Mercury.

10. *Malkuth.* A staff adorned with the three mother letters of the Hebrew alphabet: *Shin, Aleph,* and *Mem.* It signifies the caduceus, the Wand of Mercury.

The Sephirotic disks are yellow with green details, Mercury and Virgo in Atziluth. Mercury is the ruling planet of Virgo and is exalted in Virgo. Eight disks behind them approach the blackness of Earth and Malkuth. In the background of the card are eleven disks of purple and violet set upon a field of indigo, colors of Mercury in Briah and Assiah.

Interpretation

Riches and material wealth, sometimes to the point where they lose importance. Completion of material gain and fortune, but nothing beyond the material. Wealth that may dissipate unless applied in a creative, constructive manner. Mere accumulation.

Reversed

Slothfulness. Wealth gained, but at a great cost—a pyrrhic victory.

---

76. Crowley, *777 and Other Qabalistic Writings of Aleister Crowley*, 35–36.

$\left(\,4\,\right)$

Tarot Divination

The tarot is a set of symbols and images that may be used to obtain insight into personal issues and identify options for resolving them. As a problem-solving and informational tool, the tarot is very useful for bringing clarity and objectivity to confusing situations as well as for revealing hidden problems and solutions.

Tarot divination uses the language of symbols to communicate with the Higher Self, the divine part of the Self that is connected to the universe. Symbols bypass the censor of the conscious mind, allowing us to receive information from the Higher Self without the interference of the Lower Self, the ego. As tarot readers, we interpret the symbols of the tarot into meaningful information, insight, and advice.

A tarot reading does not predict the future. The universe is an ever-changing and chaotic system, with too many variables to be predicted or controlled. Therefore it is important to understand that the outcome of a tarot reading is not set in stone. A tarot reading simply offers the most likely outcomes and options based on present data. The person receiving the reading (the querent) may choose to take a different course of action, withdraw from the situation, or ignore the advice offered by the cards altogether.

Questions

A good tarot reading starts with a good question. There are a number of factors to consider when composing a question for a divination.

Open-ended questions reveal more information than yes-no questions. One of the advantages of using the tarot for divination is the significant amount of depth and detail that can be revealed by the cards. If someone wants a simple yes or no answer, flipping a coin might be a better option!

What time frame does this reading cover? Because of the chaotic, nonlinear nature of the universe, the further into the future you look, the less reliable your information may be. A reading that examines how a situation will unfold over the next month will be more accurate and pertinent than a reading that examines the same situation over the course of the next year. It is always possible to look at a long-term situation in terms of smaller periods of time.

Some querents may ask for a general reading rather than ask a specific question. General readings can be more difficult because there is a lack of context on which to base your interpretations. Furthermore, general readings often result in general answers.

If you are uncomfortable doing general readings, there are a couple of options you may consider. Start by asking querents to choose an area of their life to focus upon. Sometimes people ask for general readings because they have many different areas of their life they wish to explore. Explain to the querent that a more focused question will usually result in more helpful and pertinent information, and offer to help the querent come up with a more specific question. You may also suggest that the querent postpone the reading until he or she has a specific question or situation in mind.

The majority of questions that people ask will fall into three categories: money, health, and relationships. Questions about personal or spiritual development are less frequent but still come up from time to time. These are all significant issues in a person's life, and it is very important that you approach them in an ethical way. Tarot readings should be empowering, focusing on what the querent can do to change a situation or make something happen. Furthermore, a tarot reading is not a substitute for proper legal, medical, or financial advice, and you should always encourage the querent to consult a professional before taking action in these matters. The tarot can be a valuable tool in the decision-making process, but it should not be the only tool.

Sometimes querents will ask questions that appear to have obvious answers. People may seek advice about risky or foolish investments that are the "next big thing" that will make them rich. Or they may be obsessed with getting their ex-lover back or maintaining a disintegrating or abusive relationship. In these cases it is always best to let the cards do the talking rather than to offer your personal advice.

It is likely that the querents in these situations have already been warned about their folly by people around them and will not be receptive to further counseling. Often they come to a tarot reader looking for supernatural confirmation or support for their outlook on a problem and will be more inclined to listen to the cards than to heed personal advice. You will find that the cards usually tell these people what they need to hear and not what they want to hear.

Also consider that you may not have all the information about the situation, or that the querent may be lying, exaggerating, or even unaware of the true circumstances of an event. If this is the case, then you may be giving erroneous personal advice because you don't have all the facts. By using the tarot to communicate with your Higher Self and the universe, you will be able to tap into the reality of the situation.

Reading Your Own Cards

It can be difficult to maintain objectivity when you use divination to investigate an emotionally charged situation in which you are involved. Your emotions may color or overwhelm your intuition and result in a misleading or erroneous interpretation of the cards. In these cases, it is best to go to another tarot reader for help, someone who is not involved in the situation and is therefore more objective.

Connecting with the Universe

Before you start a tarot reading, it is wise to establish a connection with the higher powers with which you will be communicating. This may be accomplished in a number of ways.

The easiest method is to appeal to your Higher Self for guidance. Close your eyes, clear your mind, and silently ask your Higher Self for help with interpreting the cards. You do not need to be an Adept to communicate with your Higher Self; know that your Higher Self has heard your appeal and will grant you the guidance you desire.

Another method is to create an energetic connection between the tarot deck, the universe, and yourself. Hold the deck between your palms and close your eyes. As you inhale, draw energy down through your crown chakra and into your heart chakra. If you are unfamiliar with energy work or don't feel the energy moving through your body, imagine this energy as a white light that goes wherever you will it to go. Hold the energy in your heart chakra while you exhale.

With your second inhalation, draw energy up through your feet or your root chakra and place it in your heart chakra. On the third inhalation, take the energy in your heart chakra and direct it down your left arm, through the deck, up your right arm, and back into your heart chakra. On the fourth inhalation, cycle the energy through your body and through the deck. This method may take some practice to master, but it is well worth the effort.

Shuffling

Shuffle the cards in any way that is comfortable. The ability to effortlessly riffle the cards like a Las Vegas blackjack dealer is not a requirement for tarot reading! The only thing that is important is that you mix the cards well. Many readers shuffle the cards while they work out the question with the querent. If you are using reversed cards, make sure to invert half of the deck several times while you are shuffling.

Shuffle the cards until you feel it is time to stop—use your intuition. You may want to let the querent shuffle or cut the cards after you are done shuffling. This allows the querent to contribute energy to the reading, and to be involved in the process. Deal the cards face up so you can look for areas of significance within the spread as a whole.

Spreads

Once you have determined the question, you must choose a spread. A spread is a symbolic pattern that puts the information revealed by the cards into context. Positions in the spread indicate facets of the situation being examined, such as environmental factors, past and present influences, and possible outcomes.

There are many books on the shelf of your local bookstore that contain spreads designed for practically every situation. You may also design your own spreads. Many tarot readers experiment with different spreads until they find one or two spreads that work well for them, and then they use those spreads for most of their readings. However, when you are first learning to read tarot, it is best to start with a simple spread like a three-card spread.

The Three-Card Spread

You can look at the three-card spread in two different ways. You may interpret the three cards individually, giving each card a separate meaning within the spread. For example, the first card may represent the influence of the past on the situation, the second card the present circumstances, and the third card the future or outcome of the reading. You may also look at the three cards as a whole and read them as a sentence. The advantage of this method is that reading multiple cards as a group provides additional depth to the interpretation. It also allows you to use elemental dignification (see page 171) to modify the meanings of the cards if you wish.

Figure 8: The Three-Card Spread

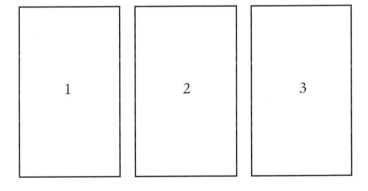

The Fifteen-Card Spread

Once you have acquired some experience with a three-card spread, you will be ready to move on to the fifteen-card spread. The fifteen-card spread is essentially five three-card spreads connected in the shape of an *X*, and each three-card group represents one position in the spread.

The cards are dealt in a counterclockwise spiral pattern as shown in figure 9. The spiral shape is the universal structure of energy found everywhere from the DNA helix to spiral galaxies, and dealing the cards in a spiral symbolically taps into this universal energy.

Figure 9: The Fifteen-Card Spread

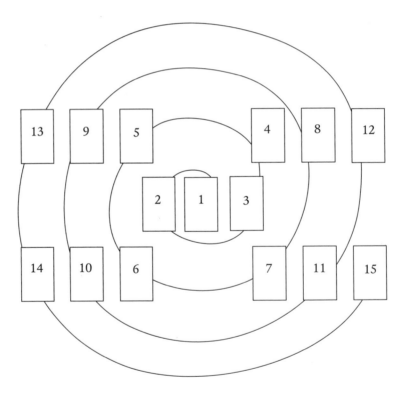

The first position (cards 1, 2, and 3) represents the current situation. Sometimes it simply restates what is already known, and other times it offers insight or a different perspective on the subject of the reading. The cards in the first position often have a relationship with the surrounding cards (the arms of the spiral), showing a link between the current situation and the outcome.

The second position (cards 6, 10, and 14) represents environmental or external factors. Court cards that show up in this position almost always represent people involved in the situation.

The third position (cards 5, 9, and 13) and fourth position (cards 4, 8, and 12) in the spread represent possible outcomes. Sometimes they describe two facets of the same situation: "If you decide to take the job and move away, your social life will suffer but you will find material wealth." Other times they represent two choices or options: "If you decide to take the job and move away, X will happen, but if you decide to stay, Y will be the result."

The fifth position (cards 7, 11, and 15) represents hidden influences and forces outside the control of the querent. It often offers general advice to the querent on the overall situation or even life as a whole. This position may even offer a third option in resolving a situation.

Interpreting the Cards

There is no specific method or formula for interpreting the cards. Everyone develops their own style with time and practice. The following suggestions will help you get started, but they are only suggestions and nothing more.

Start by looking at the spread as a whole. Are there any cards or parts of the spread that stand out? Do you see any recurring symbols or patterns? What is your first impression of the spread?

How many trumps are in the spread? Trumps in general signify larger forces at work and the fundamental issues within the situation. For that reason, the trumps have more weight in a reading than the suit or court cards and indicate areas to focus on in the spread. When a large number of trumps show up in a spread, it implies that there may be forces outside of the querent's control or the situation may be difficult to change. Consequently, fewer trumps indicate the querent has more control over the situation and how it works out.

Next, look at the suit cards. Strong or weak suits in the spread will point to themes in the interpretation. Remember that Wands represent the spiritual and energetic realm, Cups represent the emotional and intuitive realm, Swords represent the intellectual and mental realm, and Disks represent the material and monetary realm.

A reading on financial problems that had few Disks and many Cups would suggest that the issue is not as much about your material resources as your attitude and emotions toward the situation. Likewise, a spread about relationship problems that had few Cups but many Wands would imply that the amount of energy that the person puts into the relationship is a major issue.

When interpreting the individual cards in the spread, look for specific symbols that stand out in the card. They will give you clues as to the meaning of the card in the context of the question and the position within a spread. Use both your understanding of the cards and your intuition to determine the meaning of the card and its relation to the other cards close to it.

If you are having trouble interpreting one part of the spread, move on to the next part. You can always go back after you have gleaned more information from other cards, and often one part of the spread will illuminate another.

Interpreting court cards in a spread can be a little tricky, as they may represent both concepts and people in a reading. The primary way to determine the meaning is to use your intuition, although there are some general guidelines that apply. When court cards show up in the environment and external forces section of a spread, they often represent people. Court cards are more likely to appear as concepts in sections of the spread that offer personal advice or suggest action for the future.

When the reading is concerned with a particular person—such as a significant other, parent, or boss—a court card often appears in the reading to represent the influence of that person. One way of determining the specific identity of a court card is to look at the zodiacal symbolism within the cards. For example, if the Knight of Disks shows up, you could ask the querent, "Is your sibling/lover/friend a Virgo?" Of course, it is always possible that the court card represents someone that the querent doesn't know or is unfamiliar with, in which case your interpretation may be very general in nature.

Note that the court cards do not always have to be gender-specific. We all know women with very masculine traits and men with very feminine traits. You may want to consider personality traits of an individual described by the querent and compare them to the personality traits of court cards in the spread. In any case, selecting personality traits from the list given for each court card is often an intuitive decision.

Reversed Cards and Elemental Dignification

The use of reversed cards or elemental dignification adds another level of interpretation to tarot readings. Note that a reversed card does not necessarily take the opposite meaning of the standard card. Sometimes reversing the card simply strengthens or weakens its original meanings.

Elemental dignification is a more complicated concept than reversed cards, and is rooted in the idea that the active elements of Fire and Air may conflict with the passive elements of Water and Earth. It then follows that the suits of Wands and Swords conflict with the suits of Cups and Disks. When conflicting suits appear next to each other in a reading, the interpretations of one or both of the conflicting cards are modified using the same interpretations for reversed cards. In a three-card reading in which a card may be between two cards of a conflicting suit (such as a Wand card between two Cup cards), the middle card is not affected and retains its normal interpretations.

Reversed or ill-dignified court cards may be interpreted in a number of ways. If the court card in a reading represents a key concept, it is likely that the reversed interpretation will be unfavorable to the querent. For example, the key concept associated with the King of Wands is the initiation of a new project; if reversed, the card may suggest that it is the wrong time to initiate a new project, or that someone else is initiating a new project that conflicts or competes with the querent's goals.

If the reversed court card represents a person, the negative personality traits will certainly be prominent. A reversed court card may also indicate a person unfavorable to the querent's situation, such as a dishonest co-worker or a disapproving parent.

The elemental dignification of the trump cards is based on their primary attributions. The nature of trumps with elemental attributions is obvious. For trumps associated with the signs of the zodiac, use the elemental attributions of those signs (Aries=Fire, Taurus=Earth, and so on). For trumps with planetary attributions, see table 8 on the next page.

Table 8: The Elemental Attributes of the Planetary Trumps

Trump	Planet	Element
The Universe	Saturn	Earth
Fortune	Jupiter	Air
The Emperor	Mars	Fire
The Sun	Sun	Fire
The Empress	Venus	Water
The Magus	Mercury	Air
The Priestess	Moon	Water

Communicating with the Querent

A tarot reader is an intuitive interpreter who reads the cards and relays their meaning and message to the querent. How you communicate this information to the querent is as important as correctly interpreting the cards. Here are some suggestions:

- Avoid being too negative in your interpretation of a reading. At the same time, don't be afraid to tell the querent something that they may not want to hear. It is important to be honest and straightforward with your interpretation—just don't be too harsh about it.

- Always offer the querent a positive course of action. Ideally, the querent should come away from the reading with ideas for improving the situation.

- Refer to the cards by name when you reveal your interpretations. Connecting the interpretation with the cards will help the querent relate to the reading. For example:

    "The Ten of Pentacles indicates that money is not an issue."

    "The Empress appears in the outcome, suggesting that you need to be more social to accomplish your goal."

    "The King of Cups represents a person who is willing to help you out in this situation."

- A tarot reading is not a substitute for proper legal, medical, or financial advice. Always recommend that the querent consult a professional before taking action in significant legal, medical, or financial matters.

· When you have finished interpreting the cards, summarize the main points of the reading for the querent. A lot of information can come out of a tarot reading, so it is important that the message of the reading is clear to the querent.

Meaning and Intuition

To become a successful tarot reader, you must develop two skills. First, you must gain a personal understanding of the cards and their interpretations. Second, you must recognize and develop your intuition. The former skill engages the rational, logical left brain, and the latter skill uses the creative and intuitive right brain.

These two skills are vital to understanding of the symbolic language of the tarot. You must know the general range of meanings of the symbols and the cards of the tarot in order to work with them effectively. Your intuition will tell you which particular interpretation of a card or symbol is pertinent to the subject of a tarot reading.

You do not need to master these skills before you start reading tarot. The only way to develop your skills is to practice them, and reading tarot is one of the best ways to understand the meanings of the cards and to strengthen your intuition.

Understanding the Cards

Perhaps the biggest challenge for the novice tarot reader is to learn the meanings of all seventy-eight cards in a tarot deck. It seems like a daunting task at first, but learning the meanings of the cards becomes easier with practice. Most people start by laying out the cards and looking up interpretations in the little book that comes with the deck or using some other reference book. There is nothing wrong with using references when you are first learning to read cards, and this method will certainly aid you in this task. However, your readings will have much more depth and accuracy if you develop a personal understanding of the cards.

A personal understanding of the cards goes beyond memorizing a list of meanings. Memorization is merely the commission of certain data to memory. Think of all the facts and figures you memorized for tests in school, information that you promptly forgot after the test. For information to really stick in your head, it has to have personal meaning. Understanding comes from using that data in a meaningful way, by using it and building associations with it in your mind.

The following exercises will help you gain a personal understanding of the cards. You may do these exercises in any order that you wish, or you may pick and choose among them. The results of these exercises should be recorded in a tarot journal, along with any other notes and observations that may come up during your study of the cards.

Exercise 1: *Card of the Day*

One of the best ways to gain an understanding of the cards is to study one card each day. At the beginning of the day, select a card from the deck. You may use this exercise to work through the deck sequentially, from the Fool to the Ten of Disks, or you may shuffle the deck and pick a random card from the deck each day. Take a few minutes to study this card; look up its meaning, its attributions, and its symbols. How are the meanings reflected in the symbolism of the card? Meditate on this card. If possible, carry this card with you throughout the day.

At the end of the day, take a few minutes to consider how the interpretations of this card apply to the events of your day. For example, if you drew the Four of Swords, you might ask yourself: What compromises did I make today? When did I need to take the time to recover from anxiety or strife? Were the compromises I made today forced upon me, and are they temporary or permanent in nature? Record your observations in your tarot journal.

Exercise 2: *Describe Your Day*

Think about the significant events of your day, and then select two or three cards from the deck that represent those events. For example, if you got into a fight with your significant other, you might choose the Five of Wands. If you met an old friend for dinner, you might choose the court card that best represents him. If you are feeling depressed, you might select the Eight of Cups or the Seven of Disks. Record your selections and your reason for choosing them in your tarot journal.

This is a great exercise to do with a study partner or any other person familiar with the tarot. Take turns describing your day with tarot cards and then discuss the reasons behind your selections. This may lead to interesting conversations, such as:

"How was your day?"

"Oh, Three of Swords, Four of Disks, and Fortune reversed. How about you?"

"Three of Cups. The Knight of Wands finally came through!"

What is interesting about doing this exercise with another person is that you will discover how other people's interpretations of the cards differ from your own.

Exercise 3: The Book of Interpretations

Almost every tarot deck comes with a little book with a short introduction to the deck, followed by a list of meanings for each card. This is a great reference to have around when you are first learning to read tarot. What works even better is to create your own book of tarot interpretations.

Purchase a notebook or journal with at least eighty pages, and dedicate one page to each tarot card. You can start filling in your book of interpretations by copying meanings from the little book that came with your deck or from another text on the tarot. However, this exercise works best if you fill your book with the interpretations that come from your own study and use of the cards. As you become more familiar with the tarot, the interpretations in your book will become more personal and profound.

Exercise 4: Mock Tarot Readings

Mock tarot readings are a great way to gain an understanding of the cards and practice reading cards without pressure. Make up a question or a situation, and do a reading to determine the possible result. When you are finished with the reading, switch the cards around and read them again. This will teach you how the meanings of the cards may change according to their position in the spread.

Exercise 5: The Search for Meaning

Think of ideas, concepts, and emotions and look for them in the tarot deck. For example, what card or cards represent:

- Jealousy?
- Melancholy?
- Ambivalence?
- Your relationship with a co-worker or friend?

This exercise works a little bit differently for the court cards, as they may represent concepts or people. Separate the court cards from the rest of the deck and then determine what court card or cards represent:

- Your parents and siblings?
- Your best friend?
- The first person you were in a relationship with?
- Your least favorite teacher or professor?

Record your results in your tarot journal.

Developing Intuition

Intuition is the ability to sense energy beyond the realm of the five senses. You have probably used your intuition many times without even realizing it. Think of a time when you felt drawn to something that turned out to be just what you needed at that time. Or when you were faced with a complicated dilemma and knew what the right decision was without even thinking about it. That's intuition!

Everyone has intuition. The reason intuitive abilities appear to be so mysterious and uncommon is that intuition is not valued in modern society. We are taught from an early age that the best way to analyze and solve our problems is with rational, logical thinking. Intuitive problem-solving is judged to be unreliable, misleading, supernatural, and even dangerous. Thus, most people are discouraged from developing or demonstrating their intuitive abilities.

Another myth about intuition is that it is a gift that only a few people possess. Yes, some people are more naturally intuitive than others, but everyone has different innate strengths and abilities. Some people are born leaders, while others have a natural affinity for playing musical instruments or solving complex mathematical problems.

Intuition is a skill that can be developed with practice, just like playing the piano or writing computer code. As you practice using your intuition, you will find that intuitive information will come to you easily and effortlessly.

There is a significant difference between instinct, the ego, and intuition. Instinct is a function of the Nephesch, the Qabalistic Part of the Soul that represents the seat of the primal instincts of survival and procreation. It is also referred to as the animal soul, as it is a faculty that we share with all mammals and reptiles, and it is attributed to Yesod and Malkuth on the Tree of Life.

The ego is a function of the Ruach, which represents the intellect and the rational mind, the mental and moral qualities. The Ruach occupies the middle of the Tree of Life, the Sephira above Yesod and below the Abyss, centered in Tiphareth.

Intuition is a function of the Neschamah, which is attributed to Binah and represents the higher faculties of intelligence, understanding, and intuition. It also embodies the Chiah, the creative impulse and divine will, and the Yechidah, the divine spark within us. Thus, the Neschamah is the Qabalistic Part of the Soul in touch with the universe and the Higher Self, and this is the source of intuitive knowledge.

To consult your intuition, clear your mind, ask a question, and listen. The intuitive self often communicates as a voice inside your head. It may also manifest as a feeling and image, or a sense of direction. The intuitive answer to your question will be the first thing that comes to mind.

Don't confuse your intuitive voice with the voice of your ego or personality. Intuition usually speaks calmly and quietly; the ego shouts. Your ego will tell you what you want to hear, while your intuition will tell you what you need to hear.

The following exercises will help you develop your intuitive abilities. Make sure to records your observations and results in your journal.

Exercise 1: Meditation

Meditation is a great tool for developing your intuitive abilities. It will teach you to focus your mind, block out intruding thoughts, and listen to your inner voice. While there are a vast number of books on meditation, the actual practice is very simple. Find a place where you will be undisturbed. Sit in a comfortable position, close your eyes, and breathe deeply and slowly. Block out all external influences and listen to your internal dialogue. From here you have two options: you can work to clear your mind of all thoughts, or you can focus your mind on an object, sound, or idea. Most people who are new to meditation find it easier to pick something to focus on.

Symbols from tarot cards are good subjects for meditation because they are often simple in shape and color yet have complex attributes and meanings. Meditating on these symbols will reveal even deeper meanings and correspondences, knowledge that will help you in your quest to understand and interpret the cards. Start by meditating on one of the suit symbols: the wand, the cup, the sword, or the disk. Then move on to other symbols, such as the ankh, eye, or pyramid. You may also meditate on abstract concepts such as the alchemical elements or colors. Meditation on tarot card symbolism is an excellent way to prepare yourself for pathworking exercises (see below). Don't forget to record your findings in your journal.

Exercise 2: Incorporating Intuition

Developing the skill of intuition requires practice. Tarot reading is one way to exercise your intuition, but the best way is to incorporate intuition into your everyday decision-making process. Start with small decisions of little consequence; use your intuition for larger life decisions after you have gained initial mastery of your ability.

For example, you might ask your intuition, "Should I go out with my friends tonight or should I stay home and watch a movie?" You can also ask your intuition why the recommended choice of action is right for you; in this example, you might be told, "You will make new friends if you go out" or "You need to stay home and rest and recharge."

Here are some other suggestions on how to use your intuition:

- When you feel like you are forgetting something, ask your intuition, "What am I forgetting?"
- Parking is usually a problem when you live and work in a big city. When you are looking for a parking spot, consult your intuition. Ask it to give you directions to a spot near your destination. Your answer may manifest as a sense of direction, but more often than not you will get directions in your head as you drive: "Turn left, drive two blocks, and turn right."
- The next time you are bored, ask your intuition what you should do with your time.
- When shopping for a product with many different brands, styles, or features, use your intuition to help you make a decision. Pick each product up or touch it and ask yourself, which one feels better?

Record your results in your journal.

Pathworking

The best exercise for exploring and understanding the tarot deck is pathworking, a form of active meditation on the paths of the Tree of Life. Using the attributions, symbols, and ideas associated with the tarot trumps, you can create an imaginative journey in which you can experience and interact with the energies of the trumps. It is through pathworking that we become conscious of the energies of the trumps and how they apply to our daily lives.

To prepare for a pathworking exercise, you must study the trump with which you wish to work. Start by learning the symbolism and attributions of that trump. Meditate using the trump as a focus. You have to be able to build up a complete image of that trump in your mind before you proceed to the next step.

To begin, sit in a quiet place where you will be undisturbed, and relax, breathing deeply and evenly. Hold the trump you wish to work with in your hand and focus all of your concentration on it for a few minutes. Then close your eyes and visualize the trump in your mind. Make sure to re-create all of the symbols and details as best as you can. Expand the image of the trump into a doorway, and step through the border of the card and into the trump.

Once you are through the doorway, you may interact with the symbolic elements of the trump. Start by talking to the main figure or figures of the trump. Ask them questions about the symbols and energies of the card. You may also ask them for advice on topics related to the meaning of the trump. For example, you could ask the Emperor how to improve your self-control, or ask Justice how to achieve more balance in your life.

When you are finished with your pathworking journey, imagine the border of the trump before you and step back through the doorway into normal consciousness. In your tarot journal, write about your experience and the things you have learned from the exercise.

Appendix

Symbol Sets and Correspondences

Alchemical Elements

Element	Symbol	Personification in Fortune	Trump
Salt	⊖	Typhon	The Empress
Sulfur	♄	Sphinx	The Emperor
Mercury	☿	Hermanubis	The Magus

Tetragrammaton and Four Elements

Letter	Court Figure	Tarot Suit	Element	Qabalistic World	Sephira
Yod	Knight (Father)	Wands	Fire	Atziluth	Chokmah
Primal Hé	Queen (Mother)	Cups	Water	Briah	Binah
Vau	Prince (Son)	Swords	Air	Yetzirah	Tiphareth
Final Hé	Princess (Daughter)	Disks	Earth	Assiah	Malkuth

Five Elements

Element	Symbol	Kerubic Sign	Kerubic Symbol	Power of the Sphinx
Spirit	⊛	(Sun)	Ankh	Go
Fire	△	Leo	Lion	Will
Water	△̵	Scorpio	Eagle	Dare
Air	▽	Aquarius	Man	Know
Earth	▽̵	Taurus	Bull	Keep Silent

Chakras

Chakra	Name
Crown	Sahasrara
Third Eye	Ajna
Throat	Vishuddha
Heart	Anahata
Plexus	Manipura
Navel	Svadisthana
Root	Muladhara

Grades of the Golden Dawn

Grade	Sephiroth	Element
Neophyte	--	--
Zelator	Malkuth	Earth
Theoricus	Yesod	Air
Practicus	Hod	Water
Philosophus	Netzach	Fire
Portal	--	Spirit
Adeptus Minor	Tiphareth	--

Planets

Planet	Symbol	Sephira
Saturn	♄	Binah
Jupiter	♃	Chesed
Mars	♂	Geburah
Sun	☉	Tiphareth
Venus	♀	Netzach
Mercury	☿	Hod
Moon	☽	Yesod

Zodiacal Signs

Sign	Symbol	Modality	Ruling Planet
Aries	♈	Cardinal Fire	Mars
Taurus	♉	Fixed Earth	Venus
Gemini	♊	Mutable Air	Mercury
Cancer	♋	Cardinal Water	Moon
Leo	♌	Fixed Fire	Sun
Virgo	♍	Mutable Earth	Mercury
Libra	♎	Cardinal Air	Venus
Scorpio	♏	Fixed Water	Mars
Sagittarius	♐	Mutable Fire	Jupiter
Capricorn	♑	Cardinal Earth	Saturn
Aquarius	♒	Fixed Air	Saturn
Pisces	♓	Mutable Water	Jupiter

The Sephiroths and Their Meanings, Attributions, and Magickal Images

	Sephiroth	Meaning	Attribution	Magickal Image
1	Kether	Crown	Universe	Ancient bearded king seen in profile
2	Chokmah	Wisdom	Zodiac	Bearded male figure
3	Binah	Understanding	Saturn	Mature female figure
4	Chesed	Mercy	Jupiter	Mighty crowned and throned king
5	Geburah	Severity	Mars	Mighty warrior in his chariot, armed and crowned
6	Tiphareth	Bearuty	Sun	Majestic King/Child/Crucified god
7	Netzach	Victory	Venus	Beautiful nake woman
8	Hod	Splendor	Mercury	Hermaphrodite
9	Yesod	Foundation	Moon	Beautiful naked man, very strong
10	Malkuth	Kingdom	Earth (four elements)	Young woman, crowned and veiled

Trumps and Hebrew Letters

Trump	Hebrew Letter	Value	Name of Letter	Meaning	Attribution
0. The Fool	א	1	Aleph	Ox	Air
I. The Magus	ב	2	Beth	House	Mercury
II. The Priestess	ג	3	Gimel	Camel	Moon
III. The Empress	ד	4	Daleth	Door	Venus
IV. The Emperor	צ	90, 900	Tzaddi	Fish hook	Aries
V. The Hierophant	ו	6	Vau	Nail	Taurus
VI. The Lovers	ז	7	Zayin	Sword	Gemini
VII. The Chariot	ח	8	Cheth	Fence	Cancer
VIII. Adjustment	ל	30	Lamed	Ox-goad	Libra
IX. The Hermit	י	10	Yod	Hand	Virgo
X. Fortune	ך, כ	20, 500	Kaph	Fist, palm	Jupiter
XI. Lust	ט	9	Teth	Snake	Leo
XII. The Hanged Man	מ	40, 600	Mem	Water	Water
XIII. Death	ן, נ	50, 700	Nun	Fish	Scorpio
XIV. Art	ס	60	Samekh	Tent-prop	Sagittarius
XV. The Devil	ע	70	Ayin	Eye	Capricorn
XVI. The Tower	ף, פ	80, 800	Pé	Mouth	Mars
XVII. The Star	ה	5	Hé	Window	Aquarius
XVIII. The Moon	ק	100	Qoph	Back of head	Pisces
XIX. The Sun	ר	200	Resh	Head, face	Sun
XX. The Aeon	ש	300	Shin	Tooth	Fire, Spirit
XXI. The Universe	ת	400	Tau	Cross	Saturn, Earth

Trump	Atziluth (King Scale)	Briah (Queen Scale)	Yetzirah (Prince Scale)	Assiah (Princess Scale)
0. The Fool (Air)	Bright pale yellow	Sky blue	Blue emerald green	Emerald, flecked gold
I. The Magus (Mercury)	Yellow	Purple	Gray	Indigo, rayed violet
II. The Priestess (Moon)	Blue	Silver	Cold pale blue	Silver, rayed sky blue
III. The Empress (Venus)	Emerald green	Sky blue	Early spring green	Bright rose or cerise, rayed pale green
IV. The Emperor (Aries)	Scarlet	Red	Brilliant flame	Glowing red
V. The Hierophant (Taurus)	Red orange	Deep indigo	Deep warm olive	Rich brown
VI. The Lovers (Gemini)	Orange	Pale mauve	New yellow leather	Reddish gray, inclined to mauve
VII. The Chariot (Cancer)	Amber	Maroon	Rich bright russet	Dark greenish brown
VIII. Adjustment (Libra)	Emerald green	Blue	Deep blue-green	Pale green
IX. The Hermit (Virgo)	Green (yellowish)	Slate gray	Green gray	Plum
X. Fortune (Jupiter)	Violet	Blue	Rich purple	Bright blue, rayed yellow
XI. Lust (Leo)	Yellow (greenish)	Deep purple	Gray	Reddish amber
XII. The Hanged Man (Water)	Deep blue	Sea green	Deep olive-green	White, flecked purple
XIII. Death (Scorpio)	Green blue	Dull brown	Very dark brown	Vivid indigo brown
XIV. Art (Sagittarius)	Blue	Yellow	Green	Dark vivid blue
XV. The Devil (Capricorn)	Indigo	Black	Blue-black	Cold dark gray, nearing black
XVI. The Tower (Mars)	Scarlet	Red	Venetian red	Bright red, rayed azure or purple

Trump	Atziluth (King Scale)	Briah (Queen Scale)	Yetzirah (Prince Scale)	Assiah (Princess Scale)
XVII. The Star (Aquarius)	Violet	Sky blue	Bluish mauve	White, tinged purple
XVIII. The Moon (Pisces)	Crimson (ultraviolet)	Buff, flecked silver-white	Light translucent pinkish brown	Stone color
XIX. The Sun (Sun)	Orange	Gold yellow	Rich amber	Amber, rayed red
XX. The Aeon (Fire)	Glowing orange scarlet	Vermillion	Scarlet, flecked gold	Vermillion, flecked emerald, and crimson
XX. The Aeon (Spirit)	White, merging into gray	Deep purple, nearly black	The seven prismatic colors	White, yellow, red, blue, black
XXI. The Universe (Earth)	Citrine, olive, russet, and black	Amber	Dark brown	Black, flecked yellow
XXI. The Universe (Saturn)	Indigo	Black	Blue-black	Black, flecked yellow

Attributions of the Court Cards

Card	Sub-Element	Decans	Crest	Symbols
Knight of Wands	Fire of Fire	20° Scorpio to 20° Sagittarius	Winged black horse's head	Black horse, waving flames, flaming club like in Ace of Wands, scarlet cloak
Queen of Wands	Water of Fire	20° Pisces to 20° Aries	Winged leopard's head	Leopard, salient flames, Thyrsus Wand
Prince of Wands	Air of Fire	20° Cancer to 20° Leo	Winged lion's head	Lion, salient flames, Fire Wand of Zelator Adept
Princess of Wands	Earth of Fire	Cancer, Leo, Virgo	Ostrich plumes	Tiger, leaping flames, gold altar, Sun Wand

Card	Sub-Element	Decans	Crest	Symbols
Knight of Cups	Fire of Water	20° Aquarius to 20° Pisces	None	White horse, crab issuing from cup, peacock, sea
Queen of Cups	Water of Water	20° Gemini to 20° Cancer	Ibis	Ibis, crayfish issuing from cup, lotus, pool
Prince of Cups	Air of Water	20° Libra to 20° Scorpio	Eagle	Eagle, serpent issuing from cup, lotus, lake
Princess of Cups	Earth of Water	Libra, Scorpio, Sagittarius	Swan	Dolphin, turtle issuing from cup, lotus, sea with ice crystals
Knight of Swords	Fire of Air	20° Taurus to 20° Gemini	Winged hexagram	Yellow horse, stratus clouds, drawn sword and poniard
Queen of Swords	Water of Air	20° Virgo to 20° Libra	Child's head	Head of an old man severed, cumulus clouds, drawn sword
Prince of Swords	Air of Air	20° Capricorn to 20° Aquarius	Child's head	Arch fairies winged, nimbus clouds, drawn sword and sickle
Princess of Swords	Earth of Air	Capricorn, Aquarius, Pisces	Medusa's head	Silver altar, smoke, clouds, drawn sword
Knight of Disks	Fire of Earth	20° Leo to 20° Virgo	Stag's head	Brown horse, cultivated land, flail, pentacle as Zelator Adept
Queen of Disks	Water of Earth	20° Sagittarius to 20° Capricorn	Markhor (goat) horns	Desert, goat, scepter with cube, orb of gold
Prince of Disks	Air of Earth	20° Aries to 20° Taurus	Winged bull's head	Flowery land, bull, scepter with orb and cross, orb held downward
Princess of Disks	Earth of Earth	Aries, Taurus, Gemini	Ram's head	Grove of bare trees, scepter with diamond, pentacle, wheat-sheaf altar

Attributions of the Suit Cards

Wands (Fire)

Card	Qabalistic Attribution	Astrological Attribution
Ace	Kether in Atziluth	The Root of Fire
2	Chokmah in Atziluth	Mars in Aries
3	Binah in Atziluth	Sun in Aries
4	Chesed in Atziluth	Venus in Aries
5	Geburah in Atziluth	Saturn in Leo
6	Tiphareth in Atziluth	Jupiter in Leo
7	Netzach in Atziluth	Mars in Leo
8	Hod in Atziluth	Mercury in Sagittarius
9	Yesod in Atziluth	Moon in Sagittarius
10	Malkuth in Atziluth	Saturn in Sagittarius

Cups (Water)

Card	Qabalistic Attribution	Astrological Attribution
Ace	Kether in Briah	The Root of Water
2	Chokmah in Briah	Venus in Cancer
3	Binah in Briah	Mercury in Cancer
4	Chesed in Briah	Moon in Cancer
5	Geburah in Briah	Mars in Scorpio
6	Tiphareth in Briah	Sun in Scorpio
7	Netzach in Briah	Venus in Scorpio
8	Hod in Briah	Saturn in Pisces
9	Yesod in Briah	Jupiter in Pisces
10	Malkuth in Briah	Mars in Pisces

Swords (Air)

Card	Qabalistic Attribution	Astrological Attribution
Ace	Kether in Yetzirah	The Root of Air
2	Chokmah in Yetzirah	Moon in Libra
3	Binah in Yetzirah	Saturn in Libra
4	Chesed in Yetzirah	Jupiter in Libra
5	Geburah in Yetzirah	Venus in Aquarius
6	Tiphareth in Yetzirah	Mercury in Aquarius
7	Netzach in Yetzirah	Moon in Aquarius
8	Hod in Yetzirah	Jupiter in Gemini
9	Yesod in Yetzirah	Mars in Gemini
10	Malkuth in Yetzirah	Sun in Gemini

Disks (Earth)

Card	Qabalistic Attribution	Astrological Attribution
Ace	Kether in Assiah	The Root of Earth
2	Chokmah in Assiah	Jupiter in Capricorn
3	Binah in Assiah	Mars in Capricorn
4	Chesed in Assiah	Sun in Capricorn
5	Geburah in Assiah	Mercury in Taurus
6	Tiphareth in Assiah	Moon in Taurus
7	Netzach in Assiah	Saturn in Taurus
8	Hod in Assiah	Sun in Virgo
9	Yesod in Assiah	Venus in Virgo
10	Malkuth in Assiah	Mercury in Virgo

The Four Color Scales

Sephira	Atziluth (King Scale)	Briah (Queen Scale)	Yetzirah (Prince Scale)	Assiah (Princess Scale)
Kether	Brilliance	White brilliance	White brilliance	White, flecked gold
Chokmah	Pure soft blue	Gray	Blue pearl gray, like mother-of-pearl	White, flecked red, blue, and yellow
Binah	Crimson	Black	Dark brown	Gray, flecked pink
Chesed	Deep violet	Blue	Deep purple	Deep azure, flecked yellow
Geburah	Orange	Scarlet red	Bright scarlet	Red, flecked black
Tiphareth	Clear pink rose	Yellow (gold)	Rich salmon	Gold amber
Netzach	Amber	Emerald	Bright yellow-green	Olive, flecked gold
Hod	Violet	Orange	Red russet	Yellowish-brown, flecked white
Yesod	Indigo	Violet	Very dark purple	Citrine, flecked azure
Malkuth	Yellow	Citrine, olive, russet, and black saltire	As Queen Scale, but gold flecked black	Black rayed with yellow

Glossary

Abyss—The void between the supernal Sephiroth and the lower Sephiroth on the Tree of Life that separates the ideal and the real.

Adam Kadmon—The human body projected upon the Tree of Life.

Adept—One who has achieved the knowledge and guidance of the Higher Self. In the Golden Dawn system, an Adept is one who has attainted the grade of Adeptus Minor.

Adeptus Minor—The seventh and final grade of initiation in the Golden Dawn, in which the initiate achieves the knowledge and guidance of his Higher Self.

Aeon of Horus—The third and current Thelemic Aeon, characterized as the Aeon of the child and promoting individuality. Also referred to as the New Aeon.

Aeon of Isis—The first Thelemic Aeon, characterized by maternal power and worship of the Earth.

Aeon of Osiris—The second Thelemic Aeon, characterized by paternal power and worship of gods of sacrifice, death, and resurrection (notably Osiris and Christ.). Also referred to as the Old Aeon.

Aethyr—A spiritual plane of initiation in the Enochian system of magick.

Ain Soph Aur (Hebrew: "boundless limitless light")—The three veils of negative existence above Kether.

Ankh-af-na-Khonsu—The scribe pictured on the Stèle of Revealing.

Assiah—The last of the four Qabalistic Worlds, the world of action and matter.

Astral Plane—The plane of energy that coexists with the physical plane. Changes on one plane will cause changes on the other plane.

Atziluth—The first of the four Qabalistic Worlds, the world of archetypes and god-names (divinity).

Babalon—The Great Mother, Sacred Whore, and priestess of Thelema; the archetypal woman.

Beast—The priest of Thelema; the archetypal man.

Blood—In sexual magick, blood represents semen.

The Book of the Law—The primary holy book of Thelema.

Book T—A Golden Dawn document containing the occult attributions of the tarot.

Briah—The second of the four Qabalistic Worlds, the world of creation and archangels.

Chakras—Seven energy centers that govern the physical and spiritual health of the human body, according to a Hindu system.

Chiah—The Qabalistic Part of the Soul that represents the creative impulse and divine will. The Chiah is attributed to Chokmah.

City of the Pyramids—The destination of the Adept crossing the Abyss. The City of the Pyramids is located in Binah.

Decan—A measurement of 10° of the zodiac wheel. Each zodiacal sign (30°) is composed of three decans.

Elemental Weapons—The four tools used in traditional magickal work, corresponding with the four elements and four suits of the tarot.

Enochian—A system of angelic magick received by Elizabethan magus Dr. John Dee and his seer, Edward Kelly. The Enochian system is an important part of the Golden Dawn system of magick.

Equinox of the Gods—The beginning of the Aeon of Horus; specifically, the Spring Equinox of March 20, 1904.

First Matter—The original, unpurified material that is transformed in an alchemical operation. In physical alchemy, the first matter is lead; in spiritual alchemy, the unenlightened human.

Gematria—A method of Qabalistic numerology that uses the numerical values of the Hebrew letters to calculate the values of Hebrew words. Words with the same value are considered to have a special relationship or a similar meaning.

Geomancy—A method of divination using earth or stones.

Gluten—An alchemical term for the feminine sexual fluids of lubrication and ejaculation.

Gnostic Mass—The Eucharistic rite of the Ordo Templi Orientis, Crowley's magickal order.

Great Work—The union of man and the universe; the fusion of the microcosm and the macrocosm. The integration of the Lower and Higher Selves.

Hadit—The second god of *The Book of the Law,* the god of infinite contraction represented by a point in space or a winged solar orb.

Harpocrates—The Egyptian god of silence; an aspect of Horus as Heru-Ra-Ha.

Hermetic Marriage—The ritual union of opposing principles, usually characterized as marriage of a man and a woman or the Sun and the Moon.

Heru-Ra-Ha—A name of Horus (Heru) given in *The Book of the Law*, the unified form of Ra-Hoor-Khuit and Hoor-Pa-Kraat (Harpocrates).

Hexagram—A symbol of divinity and the macrocosm, associated with the seven planets, particularly the Sun.

Higher Self—The part of ourselves that exists in harmony with the universe; the divine self.

Horus—The Lord of the New Aeon; the child of Isis and Osiris.

Kamea—A magickal square consisting of numbers and/or Hebrew letters used in planetary magick.

Kerubim—The four creatures (the lion, the eagle, the human, and the bull) symbolic of the four kerubic signs of the zodiac (Leo, Scorpio, Aquarius, and Taurus) and the four elements.

Kundalini—The Hindu serpent of energy coiled at the base of the spine, which rises to the crown chakra during enlightenment or orgasm.

Lingam—The phallus; the male sexual principle.

Logos (Greek: "word")—The word of creation.

Lotus Wand—A Wand associated with the element of Water and used in the Adeptus Minor Ritual.

Macrocosm—God; divinity; the external, objective universe.

Magick—The science and art of causing change to occur in conformity with will.

Magickal Image—An icon associated with a Sephira on the Tree of Life.

Magus—An Adept who has crossed the Abyss and who has mastered the science and art of magick.

Mercury (alchemical)—The alchemical element described as fluid, creative, uniting, and neutral or androgynous.

Microcosm—Man; the internal, subjective universe.

Neophyte—The first grade of initiation in the Golden Dawn. Also refers to a new student of magick or an inexperienced magician.

Nephesch—The Qabalistic Part of the Soul that represents the seat of the primal instincts of survival and procreation, also referred to as the animal soul. The Nephesch is attributed to Yesod and Malkuth.

Neschamah—The Qabalistic Part of the Soul that represents understanding and intuition. The Neschamah is attributed to Binah.

Nuit—The first deity of *The Book of the Law,* the goddess of infinite space associated with the night sky.

Pentagram—A symbol of man and the microcosm, associated with the five elements.

Philosopher's Stone—The goal of alchemical work, a substance that brings good health and long life to those who ingest it.

Philosophus—The fifth grade of initiation in the Golden Dawn, associated with the element of Fire and the Sephira Netzach.

Phoenix Wand—A Wand associated with the element of Fire and used in the Adeptus Minor Ritual.

Portal—The sixth grade of initiation in the Golden Dawn, associated with the element of Spirit.

Powers of the Sphinx—The virtues that must be exercised to become an Adept: to Know, to Will, to Dare, and to Keep Silent. Crowley added a fifth Power of the Sphinx: to Go.

Practicus—The fourth grade of initiation in the Golden Dawn, associated with the element of Water and the Sephira Hod.

Primium Mobile—The zodiac.

Qabalistic Parts of the Soul—The elements of the human mind attributed to the Tree of Life, consisting of five parts: the Yechidah, Chiah, Neschamah, Ruach, and the Nephesch.

Qabalistic Worlds—A model of the emanation of the universe that consists of four levels, each containing a separate Tree of Life: Atziluth, Briah, Yetzirah, and Assiah.

Querent—The person seeking information and advice from a tarot reading.

Ra-Hoor-Khuit—The third god of *The Book of the Law* and the god of the Sun; an aspect of Horus as Heru-Ra-Ha.

Red Tincture—The highest qualities of the masculine; the purified Sulfur.

Rose Cross—A symbol of the Great Work accomplished, traditionally consisting of a rose of five petals (man) and a cross of six squares (divinity).

Ruach—The Qabalistic Part of the Soul that represents the intellect, rational mind, and the ego. The Ruach is attributed to the Sephiroth Chesed, Geburah, Tiphareth, Netzach, and Hod, but is primarily associated with Tiphareth.

Salt—An alchemical element described as solid, heavy, fixed, inert, passive, and feminine.

Sephiroth (singular "Sephira")—The ten spheres of emanation that make up the Tree of Life.

Shemhamphorash—The seventy-two-letter name of God attributed to the decans (10° divisions) of the zodiac.

Sign of the Enterer—A sign from the Neophyte ritual that is used to project energy.

Sign of Silence—A sign from the Neophyte ritual that is used to withdraw energy and seal the aura.

Stèle of Revealing—An Egyptian funerary stele that signifies the beginning of the Aeon of Horus and that shows the three Gods of Thelemic cosmology associated with the three chapters of *The Book of the Law*: Nuit, Hadit, and Ra-Hoor-Khuit.

Sulfur—An alchemical element described as fiery, volatile, expansive, active, and masculine.

Supernal—Referring to the first three Sephiroth on the Tree of Life: Kether, Chokmah, and Binah.

Tattwas—Hindu symbols associated with the five elements.

Tetragrammaton—The four-letter name of God: YHVH or Yod, Primal Hé, Vau, and Final Hé.

Thelema (Greek: "Will")—The word of the law, signifying the True Will of the individual.

Theoricus—The third grade of initiation in the Golden Dawn, associated with the element of Air and the Sephira Yesod.

To Mega Therion (Greek: "The Great Beast")—Aleister Crowley's motto in the grade of Magus.

Tripartite Scorpio—The three symbols attributed to Scorpio (scorpion, serpent, and eagle) that represent the three cycles of life (birth, life, and death) and the three states of matter (solid, liquid, and gas).

Vesica—A geometric figure symbolic of the womb.

Wand of Double Power—The Wand of Horus, used to unite and harmonize all opposites under one will.

White Tincture—The highest qualities of the feminine; the purified Salt.

Woman Satisfied—A woman who has had sexual intercourse, signifying sexual maturity.

Yechidah—The Qabalistic Part of the Soul that represents the quintessential life-force and the spark of divinity within each being. The Yechidah is attributed to Kether.

Yetzirah—The third of the four Qabalistic Worlds, the world of formation and of angels.

Yoni—The vagina and womb; the female sexual principle.

Zelator—The second grade of initiation in the Golden Dawn, associated with the element of Earth and the Sephira Malkuth.

Bibliography

Akron and Hajo Banzhaf. *The Crowley Tarot.* Stamford, CT: U.S. Games Systems, Inc., 1995.

Arroyo, Stephen. *Astrology, Psychology, and the Four Elements.* Davis, CA: CRCS Publications, 1975.

Budge, E. A. Wallis. *The Gods of the Egyptians*, Volumes 1 & 2. New York: Dover, 1969.

———. *The Mummy.* London: Senate, 1995.

Case, Paul Foster. *The Tarot: A Key to the Wisdom of the Ages.* Los Angeles: Builders of the Adytum, Ltd., 1990.

Cicero, Chic and Sandra Tabatha Cicero. *Creating Magical Tools: The Magician's Craft.* St. Paul, MN: Llewellyn, 1999.

———. *The New Golden Dawn Ritual Tarot: Keys to the Rituals, Symbolism, Magic and Divination*. St. Paul, MN: Llewellyn, 1997.

———. *Ritual Use of Magical Tools: Resources for the Ceremonial Magician*. St. Paul, MN: Llewellyn, 2000.

———*Self-Initiation into the Golden Dawn Tradition*. St. Paul, MN: Llewellyn, 1995

Crowley, Aleister. *Commentaries on the Holy Books and other Papers. (Equinox 4:1)*. York Beach, ME: Samuel Weiser, 1996.

———. *The Book of Lies*. York Beach, ME: Samuel Weiser, 1993.

———. *The Book of Thoth*. York Beach, ME: Samuel Weiser, 1993.

———. *Eight Lectures on Yoga*. York Beach, ME: Samuel Weiser, 1994.

———. *The Equinox*, vol. 3, no. 10. York Beach, ME: Samuel Weiser, 1991.

———. *The Heart of the Master*. Tempe, AZ: New Falcon, 1992.

———. *The Holy Books of Thelema*. York Beach, ME: Samuel Weiser, 1990.

———. *Konx Om Pax*. Chicago: The Teitan Press, 1990.

———. *The Law is for All*. Tempe, AZ: New Falcon, 1993.

———. *Liber ABA, book 4, parts I–IV*. York Beach, ME: Samuel Weiser, 2000.

———. *Liber Aleph vel CXI. The Book of Wisdom or Folly*. York Beach, ME: Samuel Weiser, 1991.

———. *Little Essays Toward Truth*. Tempe, AZ: New Falcon, 1991.

———. *The Magical Record of the Beast 666*. Ed. John Symonds and Kenneth Grant. London: Gerald Duckworth and Co., 1993.

———. *Magick without Tears*, ed. Israel Regardie. Tempe, AZ: New Falcon, 1991.

———. *777 and Other Qabalistic Writings of Aleister Crowley*. York Beach, ME: Samuel Weiser, 1993.

———. *Tarot Divination (Equinox 1:8)*. York Beach, ME: Samuel Weiser, 1992.

———. *The Vision and the Voice with Commentary and other Papers. (Equinox 4:2)*. York Beach, ME: Samuel Weiser, 1998.

Crowley, Aleister with Evangeline Adams. *The General Principles of Astrology*. York Beach, ME: Samuel Weiser, 2002.

Decker, Ronald and Michael Dummett. *A History of the Occult Tarot*. London: Gerald Duckworth & Co., 2002.

DuQuette, Lon Milo. *The Magick of Thelema*. York Beach, ME: Samuel Weiser, 1993.

———. *The Tarot of Ceremonial Magick*. York Beach, ME: Samuel Weiser, 1995.

———. *Understanding Aleister Crowley's Thoth Tarot*. York Beach, ME: Samuel Weiser, 2003.

Forrest, Steven. *The Inner Sky*. San Diego: ACS Publications, 1988.

Godwin, David. *Godwin's Cabalistic Encyclopedia*, 4th edition. St. Paul, MN: Llewellyn, 1994.

Graves, Robert. *The Greek Myths: Volumes 1 & 2*. New York: Penguin, 1960.

Greer, John Michael. *Paths of Wisdom: Principles and Practice of the Magical Cabala in the Western Tradition*. St. Paul, MN: Llewellyn, 1996.

Guttman, Ariel and Kenneth Johnson. *Mythic Astrology: Archetypal Powers in the Horoscope*. St. Paul, MN: Llewellyn, 1993.

Huson, Paul. *Mystical Origins of the Tarot*. Rochester, VT: Destiny Books, 2004.

Kaplan, Aryeh. *The Sepher Yetzirah*. Northvale, NJ: Jason Aronson, Inc., 1995.

Kraig, Donald Michael. *Modern Magick*. St. Paul, MN: Llewellyn, 1994.

———. *Modern Sex Magick*. St. Paul, MN: Llewellyn, 1998.

Lévi, Eliphas (Alphonse Louis Constant). *Transcendental Magic: Its Doctrine and Ritual*, trans. A.E. Waite. York Beach, ME: Samuel Weiser, 1999.

———. *The Magical Ritual of the Sanctum Regnum*. Kila, MT: Kessinger Publishing, no date.

Mathers, S. L. MacGregor. *The Tarot: A Short Treatise on Reading Cards*. York Beach, ME: Samuel Weiser, 1993.

Papus (Gérard Encausse). *The Tarot of the Bohemians*. London: Senate, 1994.

Paracelsus. *The Hermetic and Alchemical Writings of Paracelsus the Great*, ed. A. E. Waite. Edmonds, WA: Alchemical Press, 1992.

Pollack, Rachel. *Seventy-Eight Degrees of Wisdom*. San Francisco: Thorsons, 1997.

Regardie, Israel. *The Golden Dawn*, 6th edition. St. Paul, MN: Llewellyn, 1994.

———. *The Middle Pillar: The Balance Between Mind and Magic.* St. Paul, MN: Llewellyn, 1998.

U. D., Frater. *Secrets of Western Sex Magic: Magical Energy and Gnostic Trance.* St. Paul, MN: Llewellyn, 2001.

Wang, Robert. *The Qabalistic Tarot.* York Beach, ME: Samuel Weiser, 1992.

Wanless, James. *New Age Tarot.* Carmel, CA: Merrill-West, 1986.

Wasserman, James. *Instructions for Aleister Crowley's Thoth Tarot Deck.* Stamford, CT: U.S. Games Systems, Inc., 1983. (Different editions of this booklet accompany the large and the small Thoth decks. The large version contains two essays by Lady Frieda Harris, while the small version contains only one.)

Webster's Ninth New Collegiate Dictionary. Springfield, MA: Merriam-Webster, 1988.

Williams, Brian. *A Renaissance Tarot.* Stamford, CT: U.S. Games Systems, Inc., 1994.

Index

Free Catalog

Get the latest information on our body, mind, and spirit products! To receive a **free** copy of Llewellyn's consumer catalog, *New Worlds of Mind & Spirit,* simply call 1-877-NEW-WRLD or visit our website at www.llewellyn.com and click on *New Worlds.*

LLEWELLYN ORDERING INFORMATION

Order Online:
Visit our website at www.llewellyn.com, select your books, and order them on our secure server.

Order by Phone:
· Call toll-free within the U.S. at 1-877-NEW-WRLD (1-877-639-9753). Call toll-free within Canada at 1-866-NEW-WRLD (1-866-639-9753)
· We accept VISA, MasterCard, and American Express

Order by Mail:
Send the full price of your order (MN residents add 6.5% sales tax) in U.S. funds, plus postage & handling to:

> Llewellyn Worldwide
> 2143 Wooddale Drive
> Woodbury, MN 55125-2989

Postage & Handling:

Standard (U.S., Mexico, & Canada). If your order is:
> $24.99 and under, add $3.00
> $25.00 and over, FREE STANDARD SHIPPING

AK, HI, PR: $15.00 for one book plus $1.00 for each additional book.

International Orders (airmail only):
> $16.00 for one book plus $3.00 for each additional book

Orders are processed within 2 business days.

Please allow for normal shipping time. Postage and handling rates subject to change.

The Golden Dawn Enochian Skrying Tarot
Your Complete System for Divination

CHIC AND SANDRA TABATHA CICERO
DECK CREATED BY BILL AND JUDI GENAW

As the most comprehensive and versatile Enochian Tarot deck ever created, *The Golden Dawn Enochian Skrying Tarot* incorporates one of the most powerful systems of magic around: Enochian magic. Its form of divination, however, has not been easy to master. This deck changes that. Beginners and Adepts alike finally have an easy way to use the Enochian system as a potent stepping stone to growth in the Western esoteric tradition.

This is the only deck that contains the complete symbolism of the Watchtower squares. It unites the related energies and correspondences of each Enochian pyramid and the Tablet of Union to create the Archangelic names that rule the entire system.

978-0-7387-0201-8
Boxed kit (6 x 9) includes
89 full color cards
432 page book $39.95

Tarot & Magic
Donald Michael Kraig
Foreword by Mary K. Greer

Now you can take the information from a Tarot reading and modify your future—creating changes to, or enhancing, what the Tarot predicts. For readers of all spiritual paths, *Tarot & Magic* shows you how to use the Tarot to do magic on a practical level.

Create your own Tarot spells and discover a unique system for improving your life, simply by acting out the cards. Enter and work in the astral plane. Use the magical power of the cards as talismans. Learn three methodologies for working with the Tarot and sex magic—and much more.

978-0-7387-0185-1
192 pages
6x9

$12.95

The Essential Golden Dawn
An Introduction to High Magic

CHIC CICERO AND
SANDRA TABATHA CICERO

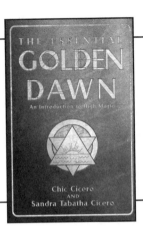

Is the Golden Dawn system for you? Over a century old, the Golden Dawn is one of the most sought-after and respected systems of magic in the world and is considered the capstone of the Western Esoteric Tradition. Yet many of the available books on the subject are too complex or overwhelming for readers just beginning to explore alternative spiritual paths.

The Essential Golden Dawn is for those who simply want to find out what the Golden Dawn is and what it has to offer. It answers questions such as: What is Hermeticism? How does magic work? Who started the Golden Dawn? What are its philosophies and principles? This book will help you determine whether this system is for you, and then guide you into further exploration as well as basic ritual work.

978-0-7387-0310-7
336 pages
6 x 9

$16.95

To order, call 1-877-NEW-WRLD
Prices subject to change without notice

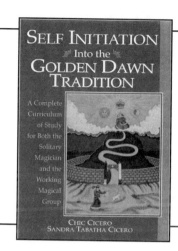

Self-Initiation into the Golden Dawn Tradition

A Complete Curriculum of Study for Both the Solitary Magician and the Working Magical Group

CHIC CICERO AND SANDRA TABATHA CICERO

Regardless of your magical knowledge or background, you can learn and live the magical Golden Dawn tradition with this book, the first practical guide to Golden Dawn initiation.

Self-Initiation into the Golden Dawn Tradition offers self-paced instruction by the established authorities on this magical order! Without massive amounts of complex information, Golden Dawn experts Sandra Tabatha Cicero and Chic Cicero present direction that's clear and easy-to-follow. Upon completion of this workbook, you can be a practicing Golden Dawn magician with knowledge of Qabalah, astrology, tarot, geomancy, and spiritual alchemy. Other than a desire to learn, there is no prerequisite for mastering this highly sought-after magical curriculum. Lessons in *Self-Initiation into the Golden Dawn Tradition* are enhanced by written examinations, daily rituals, and meditative work. Become a Golden Dawn magician—without group membership or prohibitive expense—through the most complete, comprehensive, and scientific system on Golden Dawn study to date!

978-1-56718-136-4
792 pages
7 x 10

$39.95

Tarot Theory and Practice
LY DE ANGELES

In this ground-breaking book, Ly de Angeles shares her own original ideas on the nature of prophecy and using tarot to predict the future.

Exploring quantum physics, free will, and fate, de Angeles poses a bold new theory, suggesting tarot can impact your reality . . . and your future. She also introduces Time, the god of tarot, and reveals insightful correlations between tarot and the Kabbalah Tree of Life, astrology, and the four elements. Sprinkled throughout are exercises and personal case histories that illuminate these complex ideas.

Ly de Angeles also offers guidance for putting theory into practice, along with card interpretations and sample spreads. There's advice for handling the deck, timing events, and giving accurate readings. Also included are tips for going professional: setting up a space, maintaining confidentiality, reading objectively and responsibly, communicating bad news, staying safe, avoiding burnout, and much more.

978-0-7387-1138-6
288 pages

$16.95

Secrets of Western Sex Magic
Magical Energy and Gnostic Trance

FRATER U. D.

For the sex magician, the sexual power is a neutral energy, to be directed magically for whatever purpose may be desired. Experience shows that it is very suitable for "success magic": charging talismans, amulets and sigils, and the achievement of professional, material, and psychological advantages.

Secrets of Western Sex Magic is an introduction to one of the oldest disciplines of this secret lore. It is a complete system of sex magic, in theory and practice—with exercises to develop related abilities for visualization, concentration, breath control, and psychic energy arousal and flow. It discusses the fundamental principles in an open manner and without prejudice. The dangers of sex magic and suitable protection measures are also carefully considered.

This book exposes these erotic secrets without regard to conventional attitudes. Sexuality is as diverse as human experience itself, and these teachings touch upon all aspects of sexual preference and experience. Will it arouse controversy? Quite likely. Is it vitally important to Western magical history? Definitely!

978-1-56718-706-9

6 x 9

240 pages

$17.95

The Complete Tarot Reader
Everything You Need to Know from Start to Finish

TERESA C. MICHELSEN

Teresa Michelsen's one-of-a-kind self-study program helps students develop a long-lasting, intuitive approach to Tarot reading that works with any Tarot deck! Instead of memorizing standard card meanings and spreads, readers are encouraged to use their own life experiences and knowledge to craft a personal understanding of the cards.

Organized like a study guide, this book includes study goals, progress activities, and easy exercises for exploring the suits, court cards, major arcana, and a variety of reading techniques, including methods to work with reversals, dignities, timed readings, and large spreads. Michelsen also discusses the underlying structures and patterns in the Tarot and how various cards are related to astrology, numerology, psychology, and myth. Practical aspects of Tarot reading—difficult clients, reader's block, good questions, and ethical issues—are also covered.

978-0-7387-0434-0
288 pages
7 ½ x 9 ⅛

$15.95

Tarot Shadow Work
Using the Dark Symbols to Heal

CHRISTINE JETTE

Within each of us, the unconscious holds our forbidden feelings, secret wishes, and creative urges. Over time, these "dark forces" take on a life of their own and form the shadow—a powerful force of unresolved inner conflicts and unexpressed emotions that defies our efforts to control it. The shadow becomes our inner saboteur, martyr, victim, addict, sadist, masochist, or tyrant.

Tarot Shadow Work shows you how to free yourself from the shadow's power. Through Tarot work, journaling, meditation, creative visualization, and dream work, you will bring the shadow into the light, thus regaining your rightful place as the author of your own life.

This is not a book of traditional Tarot definitions and their reversed meaning. Instead, it takes each of the 22 cards of the major arcana (the Fool through the World), and depicts its dual nature of life. *Tarot Shadow Work* is the only book that uses the Tarot exclusively for conflict resolution and healing past hurts.

978-1-56718-408-2
240 pages
6 x 9

$12.95

The Witches Tarot
ELLEN CANNON REED
ILLUSTRATED BY MARTIN CANNON

Whether you're a Witch, a Pagan, a Magician, or embarking on your own unique spiritual journey, *The Witches Tarot* invites you to explore the relationships between the Qabala, the Old Ways, and the power and magic within you. This potent tarot system has become a favorite among Pagans who enjoy rich Wiccan imagery blended with symbols from the Qabalistic Tree of Life. The divinatory meanings of each card are described within the *The Witches Tarot* book, which also includes sample tarot readings and spreads.

978-1-56718-558-4

5 ⅜ x 8 ¼

78 card deck

320 page book

$29.95

To order, call 1-877-NEW-WRLD
Prices subject to change without notice